Exalted

Putting Jesus in His Place

Douglas Goodin

Douglas Goodin, *Exalted: Putting Jesus in His Place*

Published by Cross to Crown Ministries
5210 Centennial Blvd, Colorado Springs, CO 80919
www.crosstocrownministries.org

Cover design by Daniel Davidson, Colorado Springs, CO
www.sadmonkeydesign.com

Printed in the United States of America

ISBN: 978-0-9851187-0-9

For the King

Contents

Part One: Thinking Jesus First

1

Why Did God Make the World?

"In the beginning God created the heavens and the earth." (Genesis 1:1)

Why do you and I exist? Why do the sun, moon, and stars exist? How about butterflies and mountain goats? Or pufferfish? Why are there multiple races of men spread throughout the world? Why is the world spread throughout the world? Why not just one small island on a flat planet? What is the purpose of Antarctica and its penguins?

Those schooled at Darwin University will agree that these questions have *causal* validity, that is, that we can ask what caused things to exist. (Their answer: "Pure dumb luck.") They will deny, however, that the questions have any *telic* validity, meaning that to speak of Purpose or Ultimate Objective for the universe is to tell fairy tales. Some of us happen to believe in such "fairy tales," particularly the ones told by the Author of all stories. Nevertheless, we still wrestle with the questions.

From one perspective, the answer comes simply and easily —*God made it that way.* God decided that apples would hang from trees and squash would grow on vines, and that the solar system would be a solar system rather than a geo system or a martian system. But the *why* question does not appear so simple.

If we back up a step to an even wider view, we might ask: *Why did God create the universe? Why did He make anything at all? Why not just exist eternally in His holy perfection? Why create a world that would collapse under the weight of multiplied wickedness?* Such queries are often made with the newspaper open.

It seems we have a difficult time reconciling terrorism, rape, and infant deaths with a good God creating a good world for a good purpose. If God has a noble purpose for the cosmos, it certainly is a well-kept secret. At least, that's how we think when pain and suffering are prominent.

Although aspects of these questions will probably remain forever in the undisclosed recesses of the divine mind, God has left us neither to guess, nor to remain in a state of perpetual frustration as to their most basic and profound answer. We *can* know the meaning of life. *You* can know why you and everything else exists. He told us.

2

FIRSTBORN

"He is the image of the invisible God, the firstborn of all creation. For by Him all things were created, both in the heavens and on earth, visible and invisible, whether thrones or dominions or rulers or authorities — all things have been created through Him and for Him. He is before all things, and in Him all things hold together. He is also head of the body, the church; and He is the beginning, the firstborn from the dead, so that He Himself will come to have first place in everything." (Colossians 1:15–18)

I don't know how many times I had read those verses before the full weight of their glory whelmed me like a tsunami. But now that it has, my life will never be the same. Everything has changed. The difference is profound. Its dazzling view left all other sights cold and dull. With its melodic sweetness, I have heard that which gives sound to all music. One glimpse of this woman's beauty rendered all others but a faint, forgettable impression. I now know why I got up this morning and why I should get up tomorrow. I know the purpose of blue, heat, tadpoles, and B-flat major. I know why I love to love my wife. I know the purpose for my church, my ministry, my money. I know why I should pray, sing, read, rest, love, feel, experience, move, play, eat, and cry. I know why I should live. I know the meaning of life. I know.

But it's not just about me, as though I've had some unique, personal, existential epiphany. I now know everything there is to know about *you*. I know why *you* matter in the world, why you should get up in the morning, the reason for your existence, your ministry, your money, your family, your job, your hobbies, your love, your everything. I now know the meaning of your life.

You and everything else in the universe are about one thing . . . Jesus. *He* is the reason for everything.

The Chief End of Man Revisited

At this point, you may be underwhelmed by my overwhelm. You may be thinking I'm not the sharpest knife in the drawer to regard this as a profound discovery. It's sort of like a fish saying to all of the other fish, "Guess what! We live in water. Did you know that? Isn't that amazing?" Of course, it's all about Christ. That's why we call ourselves *Christ*-ians. But my experience and observations suggest that the significance is lost on most of us.

Let me get at it this way. If asked the question, "What is the chief end of man?" most Christians would respond with something like, "To glorify God and enjoy Him forever." This answer from the Westminster divines is as well-known as it is well-stated. Who could argue with it? And yet, Scripturally speaking it is a shade too broad. It leaves out what the Bible itself states to be the ultimate goal of mankind. I should say, it leaves out *Who* the Bible states to be the ultimate goal of mankind. God's plan for the universe is not about His glory *abstractly*. It's about His Son's glory. God made everything for Jesus. Therefore, if we are going to do what we have been made to do, we must strive to do everything for Jesus. He is the reason for everything. I suggest, then, that we need to add a little something to the common response, something like, "by exalting, loving, and serving the Lord Jesus Christ for whom the entire universe was created." It will not roll off the tongue as easily, but it is more scripturally precise (a precision with universal implications).

This means that if you and I do *anything* for any other purpose than to expressly glorify Jesus, we are missing its point. There is only one way to glorify God in life, by living for Jesus. There is only one way to glorify God in marriage, by loving for Jesus. There is only one way to glorify God in careers, by working for Jesus. There is only one way to glorify God in the Church, by worshipping Jesus. There is only one way to glorify God in missions, by proclaiming Jesus. There is only one way to glorify God in politics, by governing according to the commands of Jesus. There is only one way to glorify God in parenting, by teaching children to glorify Jesus. There is only one way to glorify God in art, by creating for the praise of Jesus. Jesus is the reason for everything.

I have made the assertion, now let me prove it.

Firstborn of Many Brothers

The magnificent words of Colossians 1:15-18 emphatically declare the supremacy of Christ in all things. They exalt the wonder, beauty, majesty, and glory of Jesus like no other text in Scripture. They demand a response. They demand contemplation and adoration. One cannot read them with a mere yawn and shoulder-shrug unless he either misses or dismisses what is being said. Consider what is proclaimed:

Jesus is the image of God (v15). What does God look like? He looks like Jesus. How can we know God? Know Jesus. Jesus said it Himself: "He who has seen Me has seen the Father" (John 14:9). John said it when he affirmed that although no one has seen the Father, His Son has revealed Him (John 1:18). Jesus of Nazareth is God, the *fullness* of deity dwelling in bodily form (Col. 2:9). This is the amazing truth of the incarnation. There is no moving past Jesus in order to get to God, no graduating from the school of Christ to the school of the divine. Jesus is the complete and final revelation of God to mankind. If you want to know God, know Jesus. If you want to love God, love Jesus. If you want to see God, see Jesus. If you want to worship God, worship Jesus.

Jesus is *the head of the body, the church* (v18). This is husband-language which will appear later in Ephesians 5:22-33. He rules over, provides for, protects, sanctifies, and loves the Church. He is the supreme authority over the Church. She, in turn, exists to honor, respect, and serve Him. Moreover, He became the *beginning* and creator of this new fellowship of God's people when He rose from the dead. As *the firstborn from the dead,* Jesus secured their future resurrection hope by His own resurrection. Jesus is the cause of, and the hope for, the Church. He is the reason for her existence.

He is also the originator of a new peace between Himself and all of creation (v20). In the end, all of Christ's enemies will be removed from His kingdom, all remnants of creation's curse will be redeemed, and all things in heaven and earth will be reconciled to Him who is all in all (cf. Eph. 1:22-23). Do you see? The future of everything is determined by its relationship to Him. You will either find eternal, universal friendship with Him, or you will be His eternal foe.

But the expression which must not be missed is the first use of *firstborn,* where Jesus is the "firstborn of all creation" (v15). Here, the reference is not to His resurrection, but to His cosmic preeminence. It means that Jesus is supreme.

Our ears miss the significance because when we hear *firstborn,* we think merely of birth order. We think of firstborns as energetic, logical, ambitious, etc. But that is not Paul's concern. By calling Jesus the "firstborn of all creation," he affirms that the entire universe of created beings has been summoned to one allegiance—to worship Jesus. That is the meaning inherent in the Old Testament use of the term. Let me explain.

During the patriarchal period, when a father died, his oldest son (i.e. firstborn son) received the greater portion of the family estate and was given headship over all other siblings. This is called *primogeniture.* The famous Old Testament story of Jacob stealing his brother Esau's blessing by dressing in animal skin and pretending to be Esau shows how primogeniture worked. Remember it? Isaac, the aged father, knew death was knocking at his door. Before succumbing to the Grim Reaper, he wanted to bless his firstborn son. So he told Esau to prepare a special meal and then return to receive this precious blessing. But Isaac's *second born* son, Jacob, colluded with his mother to trick the hoary, virtually blind father into thinking that he was Esau. By dressing to look and smell like Esau, Jacob presented himself as the firstborn son. The deceived old man unwittingly blessed him instead of Esau.

Isaac's blessing in Genesis 27:27-29, especially near the end, gives a clear and significant expression of the primogeniture concept. The (apparent) firstborn son received these words:

> Let peoples serve you, and nations bow down to you. Be lord over your brothers, and may your mother's sons bow down to you.

Do you see what came with being the oldest son? All other brothers in the family would submit to, serve, even worship ("bow down to") the firstborn son. The father invested authority over the entire family to him.

With that still in mind, think about Romans 8:29:

> For those whom [God] foreknew, He also predestined to become conformed to the image of His Son, so that He would be the *firstborn among many brethren* (emphasis added).

This verse was not inspired by the Holy Spirit and penned by the apostle Paul so that Christians would have something to argue about when we get bored with eschatology. Too often in our debate about the who of predestination, we miss the *why*. Why has God predestined anyone? You say, *That's easy! We have been predestined to be conformed to Christ's image. God is making us more like His Son*. Yes, but if you stop there you will miss the even greater point being made. The reason He is making us like His Son is so that Jesus will enjoy the *firstborn blessings* of worship and devotion from His brothers. As God's firstborn son, Jesus is in line to be the head of His Father's children and rule over all of His brothers. This is primogeniture at the *cosmic* level. God is adopting sons into His family to give Christ multitudes of "younger brothers" who will serve and bow down to Him.

Think of it. You and I exist, not because God was just so lonely without us, but because He wanted to bequeath to His Son a heritage of servant-worshippers. By sovereignly electing us to salvation, God ensured a family headship for His firstborn Son. In the final analysis, God does not sanctify us for our sakes, but so that Christ will be worshipped and adored as King by a people worthy of Him.

But it's not just us. Christ is the firstborn of "all creation." The Father commands every created being to serve and bow down to Christ. Jesus is the supreme Lord of everything that exists. Anyone (or anything) who does not exalt Him works against his created purpose and, worse, finds himself to be the enemy of his King. (Remember the cursed fig tree of Mark 11?)

By this, the utter sinfulness of sin is revealed. We tend to place the stress of sin's wickedness on the audacious insolence of a creature disobeying the commands of a holy Creator. Indeed! Who would argue otherwise? Yet, when we consider that the primary purpose for all of creation is to exalt Christ, another equally damning aspect of sin emerges—*It is the height of evil for creatures who were made for the express purpose of worshipping God's Son to rebel against Him.* Sin is sin because it defies God's Son.

Why God Created

Have you ever pondered the question, *Why did God create anything?* When I was a boy, I remember trying to think of absolutely nothing. I was unsuccessful. Then I tried to imagine there being absolutely nothing, no shoes, no rocks, no balls, no houses, no lunch, nothing. Again, no success. Then I tried to picture myself being God and being the only thing that was. There I was, just me (Me?), the Son, and the Holy Spirit. I began to wonder what we would talk about. (Doesn't seem like there would be much, since we all knew everything. Plus, there wasn't much to know.) I wondered what we would do. Turns out, as a boy I was pretty bored being God (at least until my teen years). Nevertheless, there was a point in the ancient past when only God existed. Why did He decide to change that? Why bring existence to other things and beings? What was His motivation in creating the universe with all of its variety?

Many philosophical and theological answers have been given over the centuries. Some would suggest that God is a creating God, that His nature compels Him to make things. Others would argue that God is a loving, merciful being who needed objects toward which to show His love and mercy. Still others might assert that the answers are hidden in the mind of God far beyond our ability to understand. While there may be secondary truth to some of these responses, the Bible gives us the first and most important answer. The reason why God created everything was, "So that [Christ] Himself would come to have first place in everything" (Col. 1:18). That is the purpose statement for the universe. That is the ultimate answer to the ultimate *why* question. It's the same declaration as verse 16: *all things have been created through Him and for Him.* If it exists, it was made for Jesus. That goes for every plant and animal, every star and planet, every nation and people group, every man and woman. The rocks cry out that *Jesus is Lord!* The mountains clap their hands and shout that *Jesus is Lord!* The heavens declare that *Jesus is Lord!* And one day, every human knee will bow and every tongue will confess that *Jesus is Lord!* (Phil. 2:9-11). Jesus is the reason for the creation of everything.

One Purpose—To Worship Christ

The question each of us must now ask is, *Do I live for the express purpose of giving Jesus Christ first place in everything?* By this, I do not mean merely that you determine to be a better human being or go to church or stop wasting so much time with video games or be nicer to your mother. I mean, do you view the very reason for your existence to be that of *intentionally* exalting Christ in every aspect of your life? People can go to church without an intentional desire to exalt Christ. They can pay taxes, remain faithful to their spouse, and work hard at their job without consciously seeking to give Jesus first place in those things. One can even sing beautiful hymns and praise songs with eyes closed and hands lifted, listen to hours of sermons every week, or attend regular prayer meetings without a deliberate desire to worship and honor God's Son as King and purpose of all creation. Even a desire to worship God is not good enough, because God has explicitly revealed *how* He wants to be worshipped. If you want to worship God, you must worship His Son, the Lord Jesus Christ. Anything less or different is idolatry.

The ramifications of this extend to every aspect of our lives. Marriage, for example, is not a civil or cultural issue; it is a Christ-exalting issue. Therefore, we must seek to intentionally honor Christ in every marriage, every lovemaking encounter, and every anniversary gift. Childrearing must be careful to focus not on making well-behaved kids, decent citizens, or successful grownups, but on teaching children to give Christ first place in everything they do. The list goes on and on.

If Christ has first place, then everything else falls at least to second. And here, I think, is where we often miss the point. This doesn't mean merely that going to church or abstaining from certain major sins are to be elevated to the top priorities of our lives. It's much thicker than that. It means that we regard everything in life to be a means for purposefully exalting Christ, and everything that does not exalt Christ we regard to be a failure. Suffering has one purpose—to worship Christ. Sex has one purpose—to worship Christ. Singleness has one purpose—to worship Christ. Technology has one purpose—to worship Christ. Politics has one purpose—to worship Christ. Music has one purpose—to worship Christ. Family has one purpose—to worship Christ. Religion has one purpose—to worship Christ. Friendship has one purpose—to worship Christ. Theology has one purpose—to worship Christ. Church membership has one purpose—to worship Christ. Worship has one purpose—to worship Christ. Whatever it is, it was created for Christ.

How rare is it, I wonder, for a Christian to make most decisions based upon what will bring Christ the most glory? Who among us finds the very definition for existence to be that of serving and amplifying our Firstborn Brother? Every spring, I hear high school graduates explaining why they have chosen one college or career path over another, and only occasionally do they give specifically Christ-exalting reasons. Usually, their choices depend upon what makes them happy, where they will have the most fun, where the scholarship money is, where their friends are going, or what opportunity affords the highest salary potential. They even pray this way: "Lord, show me where I can have the most fun and learn a lot and build good friendships." Then a little Jesus gets thrown in: "And help me to stay out of trouble, and to live according to Your values." But Christianity is not about Jesus helping us out or coming along to assist in what we are doing. We exist to make *Him* happy. We are called to assist in what *He* is doing. And He is working to build *His* kingdom, to proclaim *His* salvation, to claim *His* inheritance. That should be our goal, too, whether making college and career decisions, marriage decisions, parenting decisions, hobby decisions, money decisions, or any other decisions.

One more example. When pastors and worship leaders prepare worship services, they must be intentional about *worship*. The goal should be to give Christ first place. If, instead, the greater concerns center on what the *worshippers* want to do, experience, etc., then don't call it a worship service. (Call it a members' meeting.) If a man plans a surprise birthday party for his wife, and makes all of the arrangements according to what will most please his *guests*—as he determines the menu, he chooses according to what *they* would prefer to eat; as he coordinates the entertainment, he selects what he thinks *they* would most enjoy; as he recommends gifts, he suggests things *they* would be willing and eager to bring—he might claim that the evening is all about her, but in truth her preferences were never considered. Likewise, sometimes we gather to "worship Christ" while all of the arrangements are made in deference to the worshippers.

Intentionally Christ-Obsessed in All Things

If Jesus is the reason for everything, then it follows that He is the reason for me. I should live *my* life for *His* purpose. Therefore, everything I do, think, feel, say, and want should be, ultimately, for Him.

Now, any Christian would find it difficult to disagree with that statement. But when we put it in the terms of living intentionally "so that He would come to have first place in everything," the perspective changes a bit. At least, it makes the living out of the principle a little more specific. Put simply, my life, in every respect, should be lived with the express purpose of exalting Christ. I should live *intentionally Christ-obsessed in all things*. And so should you. Everything in our churches, jobs, families, and hobbies should be intended to give Christ first place. We should vote according to what will most obviously exalt Christ. Our choices in child-raising and schooling must be motivated by a desire to consciously give Christ first place. What we think about, what we read, what we watch, all should be determined by a sincere and purposive desire to exalt Christ. Our every moment should be devoted to loving Christ, serving Christ, obeying Christ, considering Christ, knowing Christ, and proclaiming the excellencies and the majesty of Christ. He is why you and I exist today on planet earth.

Conclusion

To close this chapter, here is a list of things that life is not, ultimately, about:

- Life is not about growing up; it is about Christ.
- Life is not about getting married; it is about Christ.
- Life is not about having children; it is about Christ.
- Life is not about a good job and home; it is about Christ.
- Life is not about a comfortable retirement; it is about Christ.
- Life is not about fun and pleasure; it is about Christ.
- Life is not about sex; it is about Christ.
- Life is not about relationships; it is about Christ.
- Life is not about being a good citizen; it is about Christ.
- Life is not about being nice to people; it is about Christ.
- Life is not about American conservatism; it is about Christ.
- Life is not about freedom; it is about Christ.
- Life is not about world peace; it is about Christ.
- Life is not about feeding the hungry; it is about Christ.
- Life is not about sports; it is about Christ.
- Life is not about technology; it is about Christ.

- Life is not about making it through another day; it is about Christ.
- Life is not about growing the Church; it is about Christ.
- Life is not about missions; it is about Christ.
- Life is not about anything that is not Christ; it is about Christ.

Many of these things are good, God-given parts of our lives. But they are given to us as ways to declare the supremacy of His Son. To the extent that we use them for other purposes, we sin against their Giver because the purpose of everything is the exaltation and worship of Jesus Christ. Therefore, the highest duty and joy of every human being is to glorify Christ, to give Him first place in every aspect of life.

3

GOSPEL

"I do all things for the sake of the gospel, so that I may become a fellow partaker of it." (1 Corinthians 9:23)

I began playing baseball at about 8 years old in my hometown of St. Louis, where baseball is serious business. I was captivated from the first warmup throws. This love affair continued until my freshman year of high school when lady football winked at me and smiled. Suddenly, my affections pulled in a new direction. Had the stars aligned correctly, I would have played in college and beyond. Alas, they did not. Nor did the molecules of my body. No matter, because another fondness had begun swelling in my heart, reaching full-size when it came time to choose a major. Music would be my long-term love, my lifetime companion, my bride. Then I met Krista. That settled it. I would have two loves for the rest of my life—my girl and my guitar. All of my dreams and ambitions would find their fulfillment in one or the other. What more could I wish for? Everything was in order. My aim had its target, my dreams their realization, my passions their proper release.

Until. In order to help propel my music career, I started a business. Before long, I realized that entrepreneurial waters had been flowing below the surface of my heart for years, bubbling up occasionally, but going largely unnoticed. Now, they were ready to burst forth as a great river of productive creativity. This one would surely last. And it did. For a while. But soon another siren sang her mellifluous melodies, attracting me with her enticing mental and philosophical adventures. I had discovered a love for theology. This I devoured with the same hunger as I had baseball, football, music, Krista, and business. It was settled this time for sure. I would pursue music, aided by enterprise, and become a lay theologian par excellence.

If Jesus had appeared to me during those years and asked, "What do you love? What do you dream about, think about, long for? Where does your mind go? What gets you up in the morning? What brings you joy? What makes your life worth living?" I would have been ashamed of my answer. Not because any of those things are evil, but because I now realize that only one thing deserves to be my all-consuming passion. To find greater joy, be more impassioned, or experience deeper fulfillment in anything or anyone other than Jesus borders on idolatry. Maybe it crosses over.

What about you? What do you rejoice in? What do you live for? What gets you up in the morning?

The Gospel Is the Only Basis for Partnership

I recently spoke at two retreats, one for elders and one for a college and career ministry. At each of these venues, I covered the book of Philippians with a particular concern to show how obsessed the apostle Paul was with the gospel of Jesus Christ. At the elder retreat, I read the letter in its entirety in one sitting emphasizing each occurrence of *gospel, Jesus,* or *Christ.* Rarely do two sentences pass without the mention of one of them. The gospel was Paul's preoccupation, a zeal he wanted to pass along to the church at Philippi. His reason was made clear when he wrote those famous words about counting all things as rubbish compared to knowing Jesus Christ. I wonder whether our familiarity with those verses steals their meaning.

I also wonder whether a failure to consistently read the epistles as unified wholes, all at one time, leads us to force them into unintended and unhelpful subdivisions of topics. There's a reason they don't come with a table of contents, chapter headings, theological categories, or indexes. Yes, they are full of theological and doctrinal truth. But all of the theology is gospel-theology, all of the truth is Christ-centered truth. In every book of the New Testament, the gospel is the understood topic of discussion because Jesus is the understood topic of discussion. That's why every other topic was rubbish to Paul. *Christ and Him crucified* was all. A regular hearing of his writings will reiterate this over and over again.

Paul's single-minded focus is obvious in paragraph after paragraph of Philippians. For example, he rejoiced in the Philippians' partnership *in the gospel* (1:3-8). From prison, Paul's concern was *the gospel* (v7). His affection for the believers in Philippi was not due to their sharing common past-times or ethnicity or life experiences; it was due to their common *love for Christ* (v8). He loved them solely because of their relationship to Jesus. The same is true for us today: the only basis for Christian fellowship is the gospel.

One of the Greek words Paul uses in this section is *sunkoinonos,* which connotes a mutual buy-in or a corporate partnership wherein each partner has a significant stake in the success or failure of the business. The shared goal is to achieve profitability and growth. If one loses, both lose. If one succeeds, both succeed. Their relationship is defined by their mutual objective. One of the businesses I owned years ago was such a partnership. My wife and I invested blood, sweat, and a few dollars with another couple in order to create a viable company. When it eventually dissolved, so did the heart of our relationship with the other couple. While we remain friends to this day, the nature of the relationship is different because without the common goal, the primary bond is missing. The same was true of Paul and the churches. Their mutual love was the love of the gospel. His commitment to and friendship with them was rooted only and exclusively in their devotion to Jesus. If they failed to continue as partners for the cause of the gospel, he would have no ties with them whatsoever.

The Gospel as Our Priority

During the college retreat I referred to earlier, I asked the participants to describe what they pray about, what a common prayer list would look like for them. I wanted to use the nature of their requests to test whether they were gospel- and Christ-centered. Prayer is a reasonable barometer because it indicates our priorities. We pray about those things which are most precious to us. Judging by most prayer groups, it would be easy to conclude that the greatest concern among Christians is health, followed by jobs, family, and fun. This group was no exception.

Next, I gave them a quiz. I asked them to identify all of the places where the New Testament teaches us, by precept or precedent, to pray for someone's health. Maybe you would like to take the test. Can you think of any passages where Christians are taught to pray for healing? How about examples of people praying for recovery from sickness? The immediate response is usually James 5. True enough, *if you're an elder.* (Although I would argue that the emphasis is on spiritual, not physical, weakness, but we'll leave that debate for another time.) But you will search long and hard to find a biblical parallel to the proportion of praying we do for temporal things. In fact, I believe there is only one place in the entire New Testament that speaks of praying for a sick person, and it's in a book that believers almost never read unless they are participating in some kind of read-through-the-entire-Bible plan.

In contrast to ours, Paul's prayers were Christ-centered and gospel-focused. For example, his petitions for the Philippians were for their increased love for Christ and each other. He wanted them to possess a greater knowledge of Christ. He asked that they would be properly prepared for the day of Christ Jesus. When he did mention his dear brother's brush with death, he thanked the Lord for sparing him, without a single mention of any prayer for healing or recovery. That doesn't prove that no one prayed for Epaphroditus' health, but it is a significant silence. For Paul, a devotion to Christ was all that mattered. It's what he prayed for.

What do we pray for? What tops our lists? What makes up the majority of our supplications? Do we pray for our brothers and sisters to increase in spiritual maturity, to grow in their knowledge of the Son of God, and to have a stronger faith and hope in the gospel? Do we contend with the Spirit of God to grant perseverance and steadfastness to our co-laborers? Is a deeper expression of love for Christ and love for other Christians among the most asked things from us to God? If we love Jesus and our fellow believers, our greatest desire will be their devotion to Him. We should pray for it. (We will consider prayer in more detail in another chapter.)

Getting back to the book of Philippians, we find that Paul lived to proclaim the gospel of Jesus Christ (1:12-26). When falsely accused and wrongly imprisoned, he was not discouraged as long as the gospel was continuing to prosper (v12). Maybe he was simply an optimist, one of those glass-half-full kind of guys? No. All he cared about was that Christ was being exalted and people were hearing the good news of His salvation (v15-18). If that happened, his own circumstances were irrelevant.

Christ was Paul's life (v19-26). Above all, he longed to cross the threshold of death and enter the room where the manifest presence of Jesus could be personally enjoyed forever. Dying would bring the ultimate prize. He wanted it more than anything. Yet, if the Lord was not content with his earthly service, he would labor on striving to identify with His Savior's earthly sufferings. You see, for Paul, there was only one reason to live at all—to know Christ, to serve Him tirelessly, and to help others find their *raison d'être* in Him as well.

What would change in your life if your preoccupation was Jesus Christ and the gospel of His kingdom? What would it take to make Him your preoccupation?

Gospel-Worthy Living

In 1:27-2:30, Paul urged the Philippians to walk worthy of the gospel of Jesus Christ. I wonder how many Christians have never contemplated whether their life is worthy of the gospel. In Matthew 10, Jesus listed a number of things that we may find ourselves tempted to love more than we love Him. The items aren't the kinds of things we typically think of, such as money or power or pleasure. They are sons, daughters, and wives. Then he grabs the edge of every possibility, demanding that we give up the *entirety* of our lives for Him. The conclusion is: "He who loves _______ more than Me is not worthy of Me." Fill in the blank with absolutely anything.

Quite jarringly, then, to live worthy cannot be accomplished simply by avoiding "big sins," or praying the "sinner's prayer." It is a whole-life preoccupation with the gospel of the kingdom and the glory of Jesus Christ. Only that kind of devotion deserves to be called *gospel-living*.

Gospel-worthy lives will also be marked by unity in the Holy Spirit, striving together for the faith of the gospel, and selfless service to others (1:27-2:4). Notice that it's more than just attending the young marrieds' Sunday school class or running the men's mountain-climbing ministry. The gospel demands a tremendous exertion of effort.

There is a lot of division and disharmony in the Church and in churches because too many of us are unwilling to make the effort. It's hard work to show deference to others. It's hard work to leave the basis of our unity at the gospel instead of extending the borders to other doctrines or principles we hold near and dear. It's hard work to be kind, gracious, and forgiving for the sake of unity. I've seen it over and over again where a brother or sister has all of their theological ducks in the appropriate rows only to empty their barrels on everyone else's ducks, not over theology mind you, but because their feelings got hurt. We all want grace when we don't deserve it, but we find it much harder to extend when it's our rights that have been wronged. The gospel is about giving up rights. It's about Christ stooping from glory to serve us in the slop. He doesn't just clean the pigsty, He becomes a pig and lives in it, all for the benefit of the other pigs. That's our example. That's living worthy of His gospel.

Christ is the example not only of amazing humility, but also of serving without complaint (2:5-11). He *willingly* gave His life for ours. When His brothers rejected Him, and His closest friends abandoned Him, and His own creatures—men who could only lift a hammer because of His sovereign sustaining will—drove stakes into His body, He said nothing in response. There was no grumbling, no sarcasm, no quick wit or biting comeback. He just took it. Because He loved them. It's what He lived for.

I often think of Peter, the man who impetuously vowed to die rather than let any harm come to Jesus, who then, merely a few hours later, denied even knowing Jesus. He did it three times! Of course, the Lord already knew it was going to happen. He described it all to Peter before the fact. As He did, forgiveness was implied. He told Peter that when he came back to his senses, he was to strengthen the other Christians. Extraordinary! Christ entrusted him with ministry while knowing the full extent of his coming betrayal and cowardice. Not only that, but when it was all said and done, Jesus never mentioned it. No "I told you so," no scolding or rebuke; just grace, trust, love, and unity. *That's* the model for living worthy of the gospel of Jesus Christ.

It behooves the Christian to take inventory of his life, to ask questions like: *Do I "strive together" with others for the faith of the gospel? How am I selfish? In what areas of life am I more concerned about myself than about my fellow believers? What do I grumble and complain about? How am I like the "crooked and twisted generation" in which I live? What needs to change? Would I be willing to die for the gospel?* If we're honest in our evaluation, we might discover something about the sincerity and depth of our faith and our love for the gospel.

Pop culture delights to instruct us about what we should want most in life. Although there are some universals—unlimited and unrestrained sexual experiences, wealth, freedom, governmental care-taking, etc.—the American axiom is that we should want whatever makes us happy. Movies, books, songs, and other entertainment media all point in the same direction, toward the self. Live according to what *you* want. That's everything. Paul only wanted to know Christ and eternal life (3:1-21). Everything else was all rot, to use a good old British phrase. He took seriously Jesus' command to abandon life in order to gain it. For Paul, it wasn't "all good." The only good was that which exalted Christ. It wasn't "to each his own," it was "imitate me as I imitate Christ." It wasn't "live and let live," it was "I live to become like Him in His death and attain to His resurrection." Anyone who finds things, people, events, and experiences more attractive than Jesus is not worthy of Him. "For the sake of Christ" is the answer to why you should have ambition in life. *He* is why you should care.

Remembering the Gospel

Gospel-focused, Christ-obsessed living not only directs our desires, it also impacts what we think about when we're driving, showering, and pondering. It informs our "quiet times." It yields tangible fruit in our lives, such as the following from Philippians 4:

- Thinking of Christ overcomes anxiety (4:4-7).
- Thinking of Christ is thinking of what is true, honorable, just, pure, lovely, commendable, excellent, and worthy of praise (4:8-9).
- Thinking of Christ brings contented acceptance of life's changes (4:10-20).
- Thinking of Christ provokes rejoicing (4:4).

Think about it.

If our thoughts are consumed with *His* glory, *His* faithfulness, *His* sovereignty, *His* power, and *His* mission, fear and worry are forced to sit quietly in the corner until we stop thinking about those things. It's only when our minds move to ourselves, our stuff, our desires, and our plans, that we get scared. We don't have to face our fears, just face *Him*. They will vanish from the presence of the One who has overcome all things.

When we think of Jesus, we cannot simultaneously think of things which are evil, debauched, worldly, or selfish. If you have ever been near the ocean at dusk, you know that one does not tend to hold in his mind both the grand vista of the sun slowly slipping off the edge of the earth reflecting its iridescent brilliance on the glassy white-capped mirror *and* the putrid bird remains splattered beside the road on the walk down. One precludes the other. Persistent pondering of the splendor of our magnificent Savior will prevent all kinds of wickedness. And it will fill our minds with Him whose beauty leaves us wanting for nothing else.

Paul declared that he could do all things through Christ who gave him strength (Phil. 4:13). By that he did not mean that he could lift cars, win the lottery, or cure cancer. He meant that he could endure any and all circumstances for the sake of His Lord. If he was hungry, Christ was his sustenance. If he was sick, Christ was his endurance. If he was lonely, Christ was his companion. If he was successful, Christ was his boast. If he was profitable, Christ was his treasure. He needed nothing, he wanted nothing, he pursued nothing but Christ. And since he had Christ, he had everything.

Christ provokes rejoicing. How can He not? In what circumstance do you not have reason to rejoice? As a person who has hated God, disobeyed God, turned his back to God, been ungrateful toward God, doubted God, displeased God, and expressed untrue things about God, your future should include unmentionable amounts of horror. The image used in the Bible is a lake of fire in which one never dies, only burns. But you have been rescued. And it's not just that Jesus climbed in the fire to keep you company. He took your place in it, keeping you out altogether. What's more, He has earned for you an eternal experience in the next age for which there are no adequate words. The best we can do is talk about what is not there: pain, suffering, danger, evil, crying, or death. The most helpful way I know to describe it is that there will be absolutely no disappointment. In every aspect of our existence, we will be utterly satisfied. Even our imaginations will be unable to conjure up an improved situation because there the true fulfillment of all dreams, hopes, and desires will be realized. All of that has been given to you by the very God you once hated. Again I ask, in what circumstance do you not have reason to rejoice?

We are not called to rejoice *in everything,* but *in the Lord.* There is a time to mourn and lament and sit in sober quietness. But even then, if we cannot rejoice in the Lord, maybe we do not really believe the gospel. If the loss of a loved one stops our rejoicing in Christ, we have forgotten our sin and our Savior. If disease or malady stops our rejoicing in Christ, we have forgotten our sin and our Savior. If job situations and financial struggles stop our rejoicing in Christ, we have forgotten our sin and our Savior. If pain from relationships, past or current, stops our rejoicing in Christ, we have forgotten our sin and our Savior. If for any reason we stop rejoicing in Jesus Christ, we have forgotten.

Conclusion

One day, you are going to stand before the Lord Jesus Christ and give an account of your life. Every word you have spoken, every deed you have done, every thought you have pondered, and every desire you have felt will be laid out and compared to what God desired you to say, do, think, and want. He will evaluate to see whether you lived your life intentionally Christ-obsessed in all things. Like a tennis judge, He will decide whether you fall inside or outside the lines He has drawn. For anyone who falls outside the line at *any* point, this will be the most terrifying day of their existence, because a life lived less than perfectly devoted to Christ in absolutely everything will suffer the wrath of God.

This is what makes the gospel such good news. None of us have lived perfectly devoted to Christ, not even one. But before Jesus took the crown, He took the cross. He died in order to suffer the punishment that we deserve. The gospel message is that everyone who believes the truth about His death and resurrection, and who proclaims Him to be their Lord, will be forgiven for every sin they ever commit. They will be saved from His wrath. They will live eternally in His presence, happier than their wildest dreams can imagine. It is this truth, this hope, this Man that became the transformational infatuation for Paul. Christ and His gospel were the only reasons for waking in the morning and for continuing on after breakfast.

The more we realize the depth of our sin and the awful price paid by Jesus to earn our release, the more we will love Him. (He who is forgiven much loves much.) The more we love Him, the less we will love other things. Their beauty will fade in comparison to His. The less we love other things, the less time we will spend thinking of them and pursuing them. They will grow dark in the light of the glorious gospel of Christ. Then we, too, will count the things of this world as waste. We will long to exalt Jesus, to know Him, and to attain to the resurrection, so that we might see, face-to-face, Him whom we love. He will become our all-consuming passion. We will be imitators of Paul. We will find meaning and purpose and life in Christ and His gospel.

4

INHERITANCE

"I pray that the eyes of your heart may be enlightened, so that you will know what is the hope of His calling, what are the riches of the glory of His inheritance in the saints." (Ephesians 1:18)

My parents are on borrowed time. They have enjoyed long, healthy lives far beyond the allotted three score and ten. But given their humanness, they will eventually have to go the way of their fathers. Since my dad is not a wealthy man, I do not anticipate receiving a large inheritance. Still, his possessions, meager though they may be, will be passed on to my brother and me. His property becomes our property when he dies because we are his descendants. It's one of the privileges of being children.

This right of inheritance is assumed in most cultures, present and past. In the story of the prodigal son, for example, there was no question about whether the younger son had a share in his father's estate. In fact, the father was able to determine its worth while still living and give it to the young fool. Like wildflowers in springtime, a son's inheritance is not a matter of *if*, but of *what and when*.

God's Son also expects to inherit something. And, like the prodigal, He does not have to wait until His Father's death to receive it. Jesus inherits *everything*. He gets it all, literally. We have already seen from Colossians 1:15 that everything in the heavens and earth, visible or invisible (which pretty much sums up the possibilities), was created for Jesus. Similarly, the second verse of Hebrews calls Jesus the "heir of all things." I urge you to let this sink in all the way to the bone. The implications could not be more significant. Every particle—every atom down to the most microscopic level and all of the minuscule things the human eye may never be able to perceive —all of it belongs to Jesus Christ and was created *for Him*. The millions of stars, planets, and galaxies, all of it to the very end of the universe, far beyond what man's eye will ever reach, has Christ as its Lord and its purpose for existence. The cosmological and telic answers to each and every "Why?" is "for Him!"

Another way to understand this would be to say that all things exist for the sake of the Son of God and in order for the Father to bequeath them to His Son. The cosmos is Christ's estate, created specifically for Him. Angels do not exist for their own sakes. Even their ministry to those who are being saved is, in the final analysis, a service to the One who saved them. Aaron's priesthood was a temporary, *typical* ministry to Israel. Its greater purpose was like that of John the Baptist—proclaim Christ and then get out of the way. Moses was a servant in God's house, but Jesus, the heir, owns it. The Old Covenant was not the eternal covenant. It existed to provoke and reveal sin so that the co-heirs with Christ would believe in Him and thereby be adopted into His family. The promises of land, children, and the nations, which God made to Abraham, were given to his Seed. He is the final heir of everything. It all belongs to Jesus.

It's been said that there is not a single square inch in all the universe over which Jesus Christ does not say, "Mine!" This is the constant refrain of the New Testament (and the Old Testament, for that matter). If it exists, the Father has given it to His Son. The answer, then, to the question, "What's it all for?" is "Jesus." He gets the entire universe as His inheritance.

You Are God's Gift to Jesus

Consider it! You were given as a gift from the Father to the Son. Your chief objective, therefore, throughout the next hour, and the one after that, and the one after that *ad infinitum* (literally) is to be an appropriate gift. You do not exist for your sake, but for His. Your time, family, friends, job, possessions, indeed your very life in toto is not ultimately yours, but His.

I like to address this with my kids by saying something like, "Son, it's time for another astronomy lesson. Here is the center of the universe. Guess what? It's not you." We need to be reminded of that frequently, even as adults. The world does not revolve around me or you. But it does revolve around Jesus. He is the center of the universe. It all exists for Him. All of the multifarious aspects of God's wonderful work of creation are bequeathed by the Father to His Son for His everlasting enjoyment.

Someday, all things will be made new, all things will be regenerated, all things will be purified into a universe worthy of the Son of God. The new heavens and new earth will be devoid of all degradation and decay because such things don't belong in God's heritage. Only gold streets, diamond gates, and righteous citizens are proper for a divine heir. Even death is ruled out of order where the giver of life dwells. Every vestige of sin and its corruptions will be removed when the time comes for Jesus to take possession of His grand estate.

This is why the New Testament repeatedly teaches the "become who you are" principle. We have been made new, therefore we should live as new creatures. We have put on the new man, therefore we should put on the new man. We have been sanctified, therefore we should behave distinctly. We are Christ's inheritance and we should live worthy of the calling. A person worthy of the Light of the world will not walk in darkness. A person worthy of life-giving Water will not swim in bitter, lukewarm streams. A person worthy of the Great Shepherd will not hang out with the wolves. Christ has inherited you. He purchased you with His own blood. Your greatest ambition in life ought to be to become the most excellent inheritance possible for God's Son. All who love and long for His appearing will purify themselves, wanting to be found faithful, pleasing, and acceptable to Him. We want Him to rejoice in His inheritance.

So, Christian, are you using *His* money for *your* glory? Are you fornicating with His body? Are you wasting His time and talents? Are you defacing His landscapes? Are you slandering and dividing His people? Are you acting as though time, people, and events should focus on what makes you happy rather than what makes Him happy? If so, I urge you to remember that you were created for Him, not the other way around.

Your Country Is God's Gift to Jesus

What is true of people individually is true of us collectively. The nations exist for Christ to inherit. Have you ever thought about that? Let me help you think for a moment:

People are fascinating to look at. We come in different shapes and sizes. Our features are featured diversely. Our shading varies. Our faces display degrees of roundness or flatness. Some noses protrude more than others, as do some chins. Some are tall, others small. Some are thin, others not so much. There are dark people, fair-skinned people, and all versions in between. And although emigration, intermarriage, and time prevent clear boundaries from maintaining, we can generally categorize the looks of people according to their ethnic heritage. God created distinct nations with physically distinguishing characteristics. And we haven't mentioned differences in language, culture, customs, recreation, arts, and the many other interesting traits that make us fascinating to watch.

Why the diversity in nations, languages, traditions, and appearances? Why has God scattered humanity across the globe?

In Psalm 2:8, God says to His Son, "Ask of me, and I will give the nations as Your inheritance and the ends of the earth as Your possession." There's our answer. People groups and civilizations exist for Christ's sake.

The opening words of Psalm 2 find God laughing at the kings of the earth. Why? Because they are devising a plan to take Him out. Global peace has finally come as the world unites to make war against its Maker. They are enraged at His audacity in thinking that He has the right to rule over them. They have had enough. They will cast off His chains once and for all and be done with Him. Then they will be free! And finally everything will be left in the hands of almighty man to do whatever is right in his own eyes. This peon rebellion makes God chuckle. It's like when my six year-old son charges Mount

Dad with foam darts. You know, the kind with the plastic suction cups on the end? It's cute. Laughable. Silly. Fun even.

If you read the Psalm, you will notice that their ire is directed not only at the Lord, but also against His *Anointed.* They are furious with Christ. They refuse to submit to Him as their king. This, in turn, makes God furious. Suddenly, He is no longer laughing. He is irate at their insurrection. He has established His King and commanded all nations to bow before Him. That's their reason for being. He made them to be His inheritance. He said to His Son, "Ask, and I will make the nations Your heritage." The Son asked. The nations belong to Him now. Failure to bow before His lordship is cause for capital punishment of the most capital kind. He will handle these insubordinate imps like they were clay pots, dashing them against the rocks and scattering their pieces in the ocean waves. There is only one way to avoid this disaster. The nations must repent. They must kiss the Son. They must flee to His grace for refuge, kneel before His majesty, and love Him, or else face His wrath.

We who live in the U.S. tend to get all bent out of shape over our government's economic decisions, or its foreign policies, or any number of other issues. They matter to us because they impact our lives and take our money. But I wonder whether we react more as American citizens than as kingdom citizens. The truth is that many of our fellow citizens and leaders have thrown off the shackles of King Jesus. They refuse to bow the knee to Him. They will suffer the consequences in due time. In the meantime, does congressional spending bother us more than their rejection of Christ? Are we more concerned with our 401(k) than with His honor? What do our words, emotions, and actions say?

The same is true of Canada, France, Mexico, India, Russia, China, and all other countries. There is no single nation whose leaders avowedly rule in allegiance to God's Son. Why would anyone think that their nation is safe from His wrath? Every day in which the Owner of the vineyard allows His rebellious stewards to drink wine rather than blood is a day of divine patience. Someday it will run out. And who is tasked to sound the alarm? His witnesses. You and me. But we will never do it if we don't really believe it, if we're really more American (or German or whatever) than Christian.

Most Christians I know would readily agree that Jesus is Lord now. But I'm not sure that most believe that He is actually doing much with His lordship. Maybe in individual lives He does some things like picking us up when we fall or comforting us through a difficult situation or helping us get a better shift at work. But beyond that, He's just sort of hanging around Heaven waiting to come get us. That's when the real action starts. We become functional deists.

The biblical testimony is that He is sovereignly reigning over everything that happens. He is actively placing His feet upon the backs of His enemies. He is calling the nations to fulfill their mandate of being His inheritance. He is seeking those who willingly pay homage to His glory, and preparing to destroy those who don't. He is receiving and expurgating His heritage. Those of us who know this truth must be open in our allegiance to Him and warn others of His coming wrath.

5

MYSTERY

"To me, the very least of all saints, this grace was given, to preach to the Gentiles the unfathomable riches of Christ, and to bring to light what is the administration of the mystery which for ages has been hidden in God who created all things." (Ephesians 3:8–9)

The light of the Son outshone the light of the sun on the day Saul of Tarsus met Him. The brightness left him blind. That would prove the lesser of two wonders. More amazing was that Jesus was alive. He had been dead. Really dead. No heart pumping, no breathing, no thinking, no living dead. Saul knew it. Everyone inside and outside Jerusalem knew it. Yet, He was not dead. Dead people don't talk, much less appear resplendently on highways. Jesus was alive.

Saul didn't have time to ponder the awesomeness of Jesus' aliveness, at least not its scientific awe, for he had a far greater concern. He had spent a lot of his time doing everything possible to prove that Jesus was a hoax, a liar, a blasphemer, a charlatan who was no friend of Israel. Zeal led him to kill Jesus' followers, which would have been pleasing to God if Jesus had been a fraud as His crucifixion seemed to prove. But He was alive. Here. Speaking. Addressing the man most responsible for the execution of His people. There would be one more execution, no doubt.

But Jesus did not blind Saul on the road only to turn and blind him permanently with death. He was about to open Saul's eyes for the first time. Soon, Saul would truly be able to see. Soon, Saul (who would be called Paul) would give sight to millions of others.

What Paul eventually came to understand was that God's plan for history was not Jewish-centered, but Christ-centered. Israel was not the ultimate chosen of God, Christ was. Everything had been leading up to the arrival of Jesus. When the cup of time filled to the rim, Jesus spilled out. He had been hidden; now He was in plain sight. He had been covered; now He was exposed. Along with Him, the plan for His worldwide gospel-kingdom was revealed. His reign would encompass the entire span of humanity. The kingdom of God was the kingdom of Christ which included all who believe, Jews and Gentiles. Paul's mission would be to announce the great unveiling of this mystery to the nations.

This job wouldn't pay much. In fact, it would cost him dearly. He paid with his time, his money, his family, his reputation, his friends, his ambitions, even his blood. He lost his life in order to save it and to tell others how to save theirs. He abandoned all dreams, desires, and devotions for this single purpose. He was all in, all for One. He sold everything to buy this precious pearl. He lived every day with an intentional pursuit of denying himself and proclaiming Christ.

Why?

Because he understood why he existed. No longer reading the Old Testament as a Jew, but as a Christian, he now understood that the purpose of his life and everyone else's is to please Christ. Paul spent his days strolling into a new city announcing, "Stop whatever you're doing and listen to me! Up to now you have not known why you exist. But today that all changes. You exist to bring glory and honor to Jesus Christ, the Son of God and Lord of heaven and earth. You were created for this very purpose. Anything you do that is not intentionally given to Him as worship will provoke His wrath. Know Christ, His death, resurrection, and ascension. Know Christ! Serve Christ! Love Christ! Worship Christ!" As unbelievers morphed into believers, he taught them how to love Jesus faithfully and persistently. And he taught that their conversion was part of the great mystery of God—He had been working toward their belief in and obedience to Christ since He created Adam. Christ in the Gentiles was the hope of glory (Col. 1:27).

Mystery Defined

At this point we must be clear on what *mystery* is in the Bible. The word is used many times and is vital to apprehending the plan of God. Mystery is not a genre of literature, nor a type of suspenseful story where one seeks to identify who murdered the young traveler with a toothbrush in the quiet hotel room between the hours of midnight and 2 a.m. In Scripture, a mystery is something that God purposed to do but kept hidden until He was ready to go public with it. With the advent of Christ, God revealed His formerly hidden design for the gospel.

More Than a Jewish Kingdom

It's easy for Christians living two thousand years after the life of Christ to lose the significance of Paul's mystery-message. For first century Jews, it was provocative. For two millennia, dating back to their great father Abraham, they had been God's special people. They had received prodigious promises of power, prosperity, property, and progeny. God had demanded strict compliance to His Law as the terms of His unique covenant with them. They had broken the covenant and now lived in exile, victims of the covenant's curses. But throughout all of the thunderous pronouncements of condemnation, there were always rays of messianic hope. Someday, God would relent. Someday, He would forgive. Someday, He would bring a deliverer to rescue His people from their oppressors and lead them into the Promised Land. The Christ would sit on David's throne. He would overthrow all other kingdoms and carry the government of the world on his shoulders. He would bring eternal comfort, peace, and blessing. Israel would be established as the kingdom of God. All who refused to bow to her might would suffer the ultimate consequence.

But when the Messiah arrived, He made outrageous statements like, "My kingdom is not of this world," and "Blessed are those who are persecuted for My sake," and "The Son of Man came to give His life as a ransom for many," and "The kingdom of God will be taken from you and given to a people producing the fruit of it," and, most offensive of all, "I have other sheep that are not of this fold."

All Jews failed to understand Jesus, most rejected Him, and many hated Him for it. Sure, His healing was impressive. His ability to create an instant lunch for thousands was attractive. And the raising the dead show was mesmerizing. Still, what about the promises? What about world domination and freedom? What about being unique to God? If a guy couldn't deliver on those things, his chances of being elected messiah were zero, and falling.

The problem was that messiah is not an elected position. God appoints whom He anoints. More problematic still was the fact that all of those Old Testament prophecies and promises were pictures of a far more magnificent (but less literal) reality. The plans God had for His people no ear had heard, no eye had seen, no mind had understood. They were hidden. Certain, foreshadowed, hinted at, adumbrated, and predicted, but hidden. The land of promise would not be limited to one nation or continent, it would be the entire universe. The kingdom would not be for one nation or people, it would be the entire universe. The King would not deliver one nation from another, He would bring salvation from God's just wrath. His subjects would not hail from the loins of Abraham, Isaac, and Jacob, they would be birthed by the Spirit of God.

For the original audience, these wonderful expressions of hope were a letdown. They didn't recognize their need for atonement, so the cross was unimpressive. They didn't want a heavenly king, so the resurrection and ascension were irrelevant. They couldn't stand the thought of Gentile dogs eating at their banquet tables, so the Great Commission was abhorrent.

Into that mindset, that religious environment, Jesus sent the apostle Paul to declare the great mystery of the kingdom—the Old Covenant was over, pork was now on the menu, the kingdom was worldwide, and all expense and priority were to be given to calling non-Jewish nations to believe the gospel.

The Bible Is About Jesus, Start-to-Finish

Most Christians, I think, read the Bible with a *VeggieTale* hermeneutic. Now don't get me wrong, I enjoy Larry the Cucumber as much as the next kid. But their approach to Bible stories misses the point. The Old Testament is not to be read as a series of helpful examples of good and bad behavior. The Holy Spirit did not tell us about David and Bathsheba so that we would learn to be content with what we have. Joseph may be the paragon of purity, but that's not why he gets almost a quarter of the Bible's first book. One could argue that Nehemiah was a great leader, but his story was not written to be a Christian handbook on motivation and productivity. *All of the Law and the Prophets are about Jesus.* (He says so in Luke 24.) That's why they are mysterious in the biblical sense. At first glance, they seem like accounts of God's creative power, His grace toward Abraham, His special love for the Jews, His awesome sovereignty over kings and seas, His unbending Law, His commitment to David, His anger at idolatry, and His interminable forbearance toward wicked men. And all of those things are certainly true and profitable. But with the New Testament came the real Story of the stories. Everything recorded before was written to picture, prepare for, or point to Christ. To read any Old Testament text without looking for its relation to Jesus is to disregard what its Author is seeking to accomplish. Moses wrote about Jesus. So did Samuel, Isaiah, Ezekiel, Habakkuk, Malachi, and every other biblical writer.

Godliness Is About Jesus

Consider 1 Timothy 3:14-16 where Paul instructs Timothy on how God desires people to conduct themselves as members of His family. We would expect teaching about good and bad actions, good and bad thoughts, etc. But Paul says the unexpected. He calls godliness a *mystery*. Remember, a mystery is something once hidden but now revealed. So, what is the *mystery of godliness*? It's not a what, it's a who. The mystery of godliness is Christ—His incarnation, His resurrection, His proclamation, and His ascension. Godliness is not a series of laws, it's a person.

Now, let's not be childish in our understanding of this. Godliness does involve our actions and attitudes, as Paul goes on to explain. But we must never lose sight of the relationship between our behavior and our belief. Pleasing God centers on, derives from, flows out of, and hinges to Jesus Christ. Neither Jews nor Christians please God simply by trying to keep His Law. Unbelievers cannot please God by trying to be good people. Pleasing God is not about getting along, working together, saving the planet, feeding starving children, or world peace. At least it doesn't start or climax in any of these things. Pleasing God is about pleasing God's Son. He is the now-revealed mystery of godliness.

Marriage Is About Jesus

Perhaps the most amazing and surprising example of mystery is marriage, as Paul explains in Ephesians 5:22-33.

> Wives, submit to your own husbands, as to the Lord. For the husband is the head of the wife even as Christ is the head of the church, his body, and is himself its Savior. Now as the church submits to Christ, so also wives should submit in everything to their husbands. Husbands, love your wives, as Christ loved the church and gave himself up for her, that he might sanctify her, having cleansed her by the washing of water with the word, so that he might present the church to himself in splendor, without spot or wrinkle or any such thing, that she might be holy and without blemish. In the same way husbands should love

> their wives as their own bodies. He who loves his wife loves himself. For no one ever hated his own flesh, but nourishes and cherishes it, just as Christ does the church, because we are members of his body. "Therefore a man shall leave his father and mother and hold fast to his wife, and the two shall become one flesh." This mystery is profound, and I am saying that it refers to Christ and the church. However, let each one of you love his wife as himself, and let the wife see that she respects her husband. (Ephesians 5:22–33 ESV)

That marriage is a mystery is no surprise to anyone who has embarked upon it. However, that it is a mystery in the biblical sense is striking indeed. Who would have considered it the way Paul does? What I mean is this: In the Ephesians passage, the apostle presents the roles and responsibilities of the husband and wife. Men are to love, women to submit. But Paul speaks, not in terms of mere rules and regulations, instead he ties them to Christ and His Bride, the Church. Husbands stand as representatives of Christ. It is for *that* reason that they are given the responsibilities of headship. They are called to love, lead, cherish, and sanctify their wives because Christ does those things for His beloved people. Wives are called to obey their husbands in reverence because believers respond to Christ in that way. See, the greatest sin of a husband who doesn't lead and love, or a wife who doesn't submit, is not simply that they are disobeying. They are distorting the very picture that marriage was created to portray. Marriage wasn't given to man simply for procreation, the establishment of the family, or the joy of sex. It was given to reveal the mystery of Jesus Christ.

This is no mere analogy. Paul says explicitly that marriage was established, starting with Adam and Eve, for the express purpose of demonstrating Christ's relationship to His people. He quotes the inaugural marriage verse from Genesis 2 and then, seemingly out of nowhere, proclaims that his instructions about husbands and wives is a great mystery about Jesus and the Church. Paul is now reading everything in the Old Testament, not as great origin stories, moral stories, covenant stories, or Jewish stories, but as Jesus stories. The answer to the question, *Why did God create marriage?* is *To give us a picture of Jesus and His Bride.*

Any movement or individual who opposes wifely submission is not freeing women from oppression. Rather, they are pushing wives away from their designed purpose. It's like trying to liberate teeth from chewing. Likewise, a husband who fails to lead and love is not only a failure as a husband, he also veils the glory of Christ. His headship was not given in order to empower *him* with authority but to show that Jesus has been empowered with authority. This is why there will be no marriage in the resurrection age. All of the illustrations will become reality. We won't need the picture of Christ and His Bride because we will be His bride in living color and three dimensions.

So, wives, submit to your husband with joy, as to the Lord, as an expression of giving Him first place in everything. Husbands, be Christ to your wife and give her a foretaste of the security, hope, and delight that will be hers when she joins to her ultimate Husband. And I will say in passing that Christians should enjoy the most pleasurable sexual experiences possible, because sex, too, is a mystery. It is given to anticipate our bliss throughout our eternal wedding night with Christ. (We will explore marriage further in a later chapter.)

Conclusion

Other biblical questions should be answered similarly: *Why did God create fathers and sons?* To give us a picture of Himself and His Son. *Why did He save Noah in the ark?* To portray the salvation Jesus would bring (also portrayed in the waters of baptism). *Why did He command Abraham to kill his only son?* To anticipate Himself killing His. *Why did He establish the temple, priesthood, and sacrificial system?* To foreshadow Jesus, the ultimate temple, priest, and sacrifice. When you understand the meta-narrative underlying all other narratives, it changes the way you read them. As this great mystery became more clear to Paul, his understanding of the events and characters of the Old Testament took on a whole new dimension. Everything was now to be understood by how it related to Jesus.

When you read the Old Testament, what do you seek? Do you read hoping to learn something about God? Do you look for examples of how to be a better person? Do you want scriptural support for your favorite doctrines? Do you need a "word from God" for your life today? If you are interested in what *God* wants you to find, you will seek, above all, to discover Jesus. The Bible is not about you, or the Jews, or good living, except as they relate to Him. It's important to get this right, just ask Saul of Tarsus. His misunderstanding and misapplication of God's plan led to his murdering of God's people. What might it be leading you to?

6

KINGDOM

"Truly I say to you, there are some of those who are standing here who will not taste death until they see the Son of Man coming in His kingdom." (Matthew 16:28)

It was springtime, 2011, and the world was captivated by the marriage of England's Prince William to Princess Kate. The hoopla had begun months before the wedding ceremony. News websites dedicated their pages to it, magazines their covers stories, late-night talk-show hosts their opening monologues. It took on almost fairy tale status by the time of the actual event, even by those far away and socially unaffected by it.

So strong was this international love affair that American comedian Jerry Seinfeld found himself under scorn after having the audacity to tell a British reporter what he thought about the whole thing. He suggested that it was all just a show, that the British love to play dress-up and pretend that their royalty has real substance. In reality, he said, it was all just make-believe nonsense. His sentiments provoked pages of heated retort in the comments section of one website I read.

But it was the response of an American commenter that arrested my attention. He fired back at the English defenders by claiming that the Brits don't understand the mindset of the U.S. We are independent people who refuse to submit to any king, he asserted, that is why we rebelled against England centuries ago. And that is why we will rebel against anyone who dares to exercise rule over us. America is the land of the *free*.

Such a bold declaration of autonomy is neither unique nor rare. Human nature, it seems, universally rejects the claims of others to rule over us. Even the princess-to-be expressed her *self*-rule when she refused to take the traditional marriage vows of submission and obedience to William, though they had been used in the British wedding liturgy for centuries. She would love her husband, she would not be under his authority. *She* would be the king of her life. That's the way most people think.

God thinks differently.

Jesus Is Your King . . . Today

In Luke 22:29, Jesus told the apostles about the kingdom His Father had promised Him. Although not reflected in the English translations, He used a Greek word (*diatithemi*) which speaks of making a covenant. Sometime in the past, probably prior to creation, God the Father made a covenant with God the Son to establish a kingdom for Him. Someday, Jesus would have subjects over which to rule and reign, citizens to fill His monarchy and do His bidding. It was an oath from His almighty Father. It could not not come to pass.

When John the Baptist appeared to announce the coming of Christ, he said it this way: "The kingdom is at hand." Jesus picked up the same language Himself. On one occasion, speaking to the rich, young ruler, He said, "The kingdom is not far from you." What did this mean? Simply that the kingdom was near because *the King* was near. Wherever Jesus is, the kingdom of God is.

The point? Jesus is ruling *now*. He sits, currently, at the right hand of the Father reigning over all things. He has been granted authority over heaven and earth now. The whole world *is* the kingdom of Jesus Christ. Certainly, the unopposed, consummated kingdom is future, but we must not forget or minimize the nowness of it.

Who are the citizens of His kingdom? Every human being ever created. Every man, woman, and child is created to be a loyal subject to the throne of King Jesus. That means that you and I belong to Him.

Obviously, many humans reject Jesus as king and will suffer the deserved consequences. Yet, too often Christians forget that we have a King, that we have been purchased, that we do not belong to ourselves, that we are *owned*. In our confession, "Jesus is Lord!" we declare Him to be our king, our authority, our sovereign ruler. It does not do, then, to regard Him as our advisor, our insurance agent, or our cheerleader. There may be a sense in which He is all of those things, but He is much, much more. His wish must be our command, and His command our wish. He deserves our unwavering allegiance and obedience because He is our King today.

Jesus, the King of Every Nation

Jesus is called "King of kings" and "Lord of lords." Consider the significance of those appellations. They imply that other kings and lords exist. They do because God created nations and governments. And with nations and governments come national rulers. So, for a man to become the leader of a country fits the divine design for the world. But the designed purpose for each and every leader is to bring his kingdom under the rule of Jesus, the Highest King.

This is not the same thing as saying that nations should govern according to Judeo-Christian standards, a conclusion driven more by systematic theology than by exegesis. Moral behavior is not the goal, *intentional devotion to God's Son* is. The latter will always lead to the former, but the difference lies in the motivation. A citizen may obey the laws of the land in order to stay out of jail, but that is not the same thing as obeying the Law-giver for the sake of love and duty.

For Americans, this should impact, among other things, the way we vote. We may be tempted to vote for our bank account's benefit. Or maybe a particular political issue reaches up out of the booth with a red highlighter marking our ballot with all of its supporting nominees. Or maybe we affiliate with a certain political party and sense the need to remain loyal to its cause. Whatever else competes for our allegiance, our highest loyalty must be to our King. We should vote for the candidate who consciously seeks to bring America under the rule of Christ because the U.S. does not exist merely to be a protector of freedom and democracy, or a pioneer in technology, or a champion of free-market economics. It exists to bring glory to Jesus.

Living in Jesus' Kingdom

According to the apostle Paul, the kingdom of Christ is righteousness, peace, and joy in the Holy Spirit (Rom. 14:17). Therefore, in honor of our King, we should:

- Diligently and willingly strive to obey His commandments.

- Declare His message of peace with men and seek to be at peace with men.
- Be the most joyful people on the planet.

Jesus cares about our obedience (righteousness). In His kingdom, He expects people to pursue what is right in *His* eyes. Thankfully, His law is not hard or burdensome, but easy and light. He commands us to love Him and others.

He also cares about our relationships with Him and with others (peace). Good citizens of His kingdom do not stir up trouble. They serve. They bless. They give. And, they live in light of His affectionate grace.

He expects gladness (joy) to characterize those who have tasted His goodness. Kingdom joy is not a carnal, ephemeral, pleasured, experience-made happiness, but a profound delight created by God's Spirit. If we find our joy in the Lord Jesus, who does not fail or change, we will never be disappointed or despairing. No matter what happens, we are always and forever people who deserve Hell but have been given Heaven.

Do righteousness, peace, and joy in the Holy Spirit characterize your life? What percentage of your time, thinking, spending, and working is given to these things? Are you a faithful citizen of His kingdom.

Every Day of Your Life Belongs to Him

If Jesus is king, then there is no such thing as "free time." Jesus owns it all, every nanosecond. Moreover, He is the King of every stage of life. Take singles, for example. The American view of the young unmarried person, say, in college or just out, sees a time of unattached, uncommitted freedom to have fun before the burden of responsibility falls on their shoulders.

Enjoy the good life now, we say, because the next time you have this freedom, you'll be too tired and old to take advantage of it.

Such thinking is too pessimistic and dull for the "times of responsibility." But more importantly, it is too unChristian for all times. The single person is free from domestic duties, but not from *dominion* duties. He or she is still the subject of King Jesus, still bound to spend every moment intentionally Christ-obsessed in all things. It could be reasonably argued that unmarried individuals should have more robust ministry objectives than marrieds because of the amount of energy and "free time" at their disposal. A truly *Christian* perspective of the typical twenty-something would see a great, God-sized ambition to serve the King. (We'll consider this in greater detail later.)

Nor is retirement a Christ-honoring concept. I don't mean retirement from one's employment. I mean the ideal of RV-ing around the country (or the world) emptying the storehouses you filled during all those hard years of working for the man. We think we deserve it. We don't. Rather, we are slaves to our Master who claims every breath down to the Final Exhale. Retirement from the job, for the healthy person, should be seen as an opportunity for more effective contribution to the kingdom of Christ.

Conclusion

Do you remember how the book of Acts ends? It doesn't, at least not the way most do. Luke gave us the most profound non-conclusion ever. There's no "the end" or "and they all lived happily ever after," just Paul imprisoned at Rome. But it's not his location that matters, it's his message. He was boldly proclaiming the kingdom of God. His part in the story was over, but the Story he was telling wasn't. It had really only just begun. We're still living it. We're still telling it. We're in Acts 29. And our call is the same: to boldly proclaim the kingdom of God.

7

CONSUMMATION

"For the grace of God has appeared, bringing salvation to all men instructing us to deny ungodliness and worldly desires and to live sensibly, righteously and godly in the present age, looking for the blessed hope and the appearing of the glory of our great God and Savior, Christ Jesus, who gave Himself for us to redeem us from every lawless deed, and to purify for Himself a people for His own possession, zealous for good deeds." (Titus 2:11–14)

I am writing this on the night before what Harold Camping has predicted to be the return of Christ and the end the world. If you are reading it, he was wrong. But someday, the prediction won't be wrong. Someday, Jesus will return. Someday, Jesus will reign, uncontested, over the entire universe. On that day, everything will be turned right again. The curse will be the only thing cursed. Sin will be but a memory. Disappointment will disappear forever. Death will die.

We call that day *The Consummation.*

Why the World Turns

In the marvelous sentence we know as Ephesians 1:3-14, the Scripture declares that all things are "summed up" in Christ. The language expresses a plan or purpose. God's plan for the entire universe was to bring it all together under one head, His Son, Jesus (cf. 1:22-23). *Everything* is united together in Him. *He* is the consummation of all things. *He* is where everything is heading.

To put it another way, Jesus is the story God has been telling since He first created the heavens and the earth. The Old Testament in its entirety is about God's Son. He is the second Adam, the priest of Melchizedek's order, the seed of Abraham, the true Israel, the new Moses, and the son of David. He is the ark, the law-giver, the temple, the Sabbath rest, the prophet, and the fulfillment. He is the skin which covered Adam and Eve, the lamb of God who takes away the sin of the world, and the final sacrifice. Jesus is the story of the Old Testament.

He is also the story of the New Testament. He is Lord over heaven and earth who actively extends His kingdom into every tribe, tongue, and nation. He is Lord of all. Someday, every human being will bow before Him declaring His lordship and kingdom. Regardless of their prior confession, on that day there will be no skeptics, no unbelievers, and no deniers. All will see and know that Jesus is Lord. Since the beginning of creation, everything has been heading toward that glorious, consummating Day of the Lord Jesus.

Herein is the universal philosophy of history: God created time and space, the universe and the world. He promised and prepared for the arrival of His Son to earth. In the fulness of time, He sent His Son into the world as a man. Jesus fulfilled the previous promises and made atonement for sin. He rose from the dead. He sent missionaries into the world to call all nations to faith and obedience. He ascended to the throne of the universe. One day, He will return to consummate His kingdom and judge all who oppose Him.

Jesus is why the world turns.

Anno Domini

It used to be common to include the letters *A.D.* when writing the year (e.g. 2011 A.D.). Most people today would object to using it on public documents because it stands for the Latin phrase, "year of our Lord [Jesus]."

Many people don't know what it means. For that matter, many people don't know why we are counting years at all. Test me this winter. On New Year's Eve, ask your non-Christian friends what year we are entering. Then ask them, "Two thousand years since what?" The entire western world has been counting the years since the establishment of the kingdom of Jesus Christ (A.D.), and yet the majority of those who count either don't know or don't care why. New Year's is just another reason to have a party.

In earlier days, people cared. They eagerly acknowledged the reign of His Majesty, the Lord Jesus, and eagerly anticipated His consummating return. It was a pronouncement of joy to declare the "year of our Lord." Those days are gone. But whether people believe it or not, truth is true. This is the year of the Lord Jesus Christ.

The End Will Come

God is in the process of placing all things under the feet of Jesus. He is actively building His Church and crushing His enemies. His wake-up calls ring throughout the world every single day with each tragedy, hostility, and death. You see, in the final analysis, there is no such thing as a *natural* disaster.

They're all super-natural. The ominous horsemen of Revelation 6 ride throughout the lands, bearing the seal of their Master, sounding the alarm to all survivors: "Today may be *the* day. Are you prepared to meet your King? Have you loved Him? Have you obeyed Him? Will you welcome Him? Or will you cry out for the mountains to crush you before He does?"

The day is coming when the Father will issue the authorizing nod releasing the Son to finish what He began over two thousand years ago. The king will return from his far off journeys to see who has been faithful and true. The elder brother will inherit his vast estate and receive the worship of his younger siblings. The husband will take his bride into his chambers and at long last consummate their eternal marriage. The glorious end for which God created the world will finally arrive. The day is coming.

Therefore, religion must not be man-centered, it must be Christ-centered. Missions must not be man-centered, denomination-centered, or welfare-centered; it must be Christ-centered. Everything must be Christ-centered: science, philosophy, theology, school systems, homeschooling, church-planting, book writing, song writing, painting, sculpting, family planning, vacation planning . . . *everything*. Nothing exists "just because."

Jesus divided the world into two groups: *those for Him* and *those against Him*. Nothing is neutral. Not even Switzerland. Everything is either intentionally obsessed with glorifying Christ or it is not. Every person is either in the kingdom of darkness or in the kingdom of the beloved Son.

Consequently, the Church should boldly proclaim the gospel in the midst of the kingdom of darkness because the King has come. He will win, for it is His destiny. And He cannot lose even one whom the Father has given to Him. On that Day, dying becomes living, ending becomes beginning, mourning becomes dancing, crying becomes laughing, suffering becomes glory. It will all happen at the consummation.

Being Intentionally Christ-Obsessed in All Things

Knowing that the entire universe is heading toward the day of consummation should transform *today* into a day of anticipation. Our hopes, dreams, and plans should reflect God's purpose to unite all things in Christ. I'm not so much thinking of dinner plans for Friday night (although, I suppose truly eating and drinking to the glory of God would include pondering the coming consummation feast of Jesus Christ.). But the trajectory of our life goals and purposes should point toward what will bring Christ the most glory.

I know a family with extra living accommodations in their house. They regularly open it for missionaries on home assignment. This is not unique to them. You probably know people who do that. Maybe you have done the same yourself. What impresses me is how intentional they are in having it occupied. They believe that if it's not being used for such purposes, there's no point in having it. A few months ago they purchased a cabin in the nearby Rocky Mountains. Their perspective for it is the same. If Christian families, ministries, ministers, missionaries, or *somebody* is not using it for refreshment for their service to the King, then it's wasted space. Yes, it's beautiful, delightful, and restful, but most of all it's profitable for exalting Christ.

I recently met a man whose business has made him very wealthy. He retired, but before long found himself back at it. This go around, things appear ready to explode, bringing exponential profits. He plans to handle this success the way he handled it before. He and his wife have established their "finish line," the amount of money they want to live on. Everything beyond that is given to building Christ's kingdom. Contrast that with Bill Gates and Warren Buffet who have given away billions to charities which are not specifically pursuing Christ's exaltation. The latter are missing the God-given point of their wealth.

A young man I know entered the Air Force specifically to study dentistry so that he would have a needed skill that would open doors for overseas missions. Six years in the American military to prepare for a lifetime of Christian military.

I know a woman who after flirting with romance decided that her life would be better spent if she remained single. It would give her more time to devote to serving the administrative endeavors of a world-wide missions organization.

One well-known pastor tells of how he used to allow his daughter to invite as many people over as she wanted to on Friday nights. The only stipulation was that none of them could be Christians. The family wanted their home to be an inviting place for adolescents to hear the gospel of Jesus Christ.

The examples could multiply, but this is enough. The arc of the lives of these families and individuals are purposefully shaped into a pattern which brings Christ glory. Major decisions were made for the express outcome of serving Him. They are intentionally Christ-obsessed.

Getting Ready to Consummate

Think of the implications for ethics. If you knew that tomorrow would bring a major catastrophe, you would get ready for it today. You would gather food, water, and other necessary things. You would seek protection. You would warn others. You would proactively pursue the appropriate preparations for such an event.

If I believed there was any biblical reason to trust Harold Camping's prediction of Christ's return, I would not be taking the time to write this book. On the other hand, because I believe that Christ *will* return one day, I am writing it, with the hope that you will be well-prepared for His Day. It will happen. It's God's final destiny for the created order as we know it. The question we must ask then is, *Am I ready for that day?*

Have you ever noticed what all of the New Testament's end-times passages are really about? We tend to be preoccupied with the timing, events, signs, and so on. But in every case, the greater biblical weight lies in the call to be ready, to be prepared, to have our oil stored and lamps trimmed, to be on the lookout as if for a thief, to be awake and alert, to be soberly working hard when the Master returns. We are told to eagerly look for His appearing, not by staring at the stars, but by denying sin and worldliness, and by living sensibly and righteously in this age (Titus 2:11-13). We prepare for the *future* day of Christ by serving Him faithfully *now*.

But too often a Christian's sanctification is driven by moralism or competition or guilt, like a child who only obeys his father out of duty. It's better than disobedience, but it falls far short of the desired outcome. Parents want their kids to obey because of a loving desire to please them. Similarly, there is a world of difference to a husband when his wife wants to bless him sexually because she loves him versus when she does it out of sheer duty. Believers who understand their created purpose to exalt Christ will obey Him purely out of a desire to make Him happy. They will want to please Him because of who He is.

I will never forget the first time I saw my soon-to-be wife on our wedding day. I wept as she glided down the center aisle. She was the most beautiful woman I had ever seen. Part of her beauty was that she was about to be mine and part was that she had made herself beautiful just for me. It wasn't for the pictures or the audience or the joy of feeling good about herself. It was for me. She wanted to be more beautiful than ever when she gave herself to me. As the Bride of Christ, believers should strive for good works with precisely the same motivation. Our pursuit of righteousness is not box-checking or rule-following or law-keeping, it is our bridal gown as we anticipate the consummation of our marriage to Jesus (Rev. 19:7-8). We seek godliness as preparation for our union with Christ. Think about how much "getting made up" is required in order to be ready for a Saturday afternoon wedding. Long before the day arrives, measurements are taken, material is ordered and altered, refinements are made. Then, on the day itself, hours of makeup, hairstyling, and dressing take precedent over everything else, including sleeping and eating. The bride wants to look her best for her groom. So should be our motivation for righteousness.

Do you see how this is not the same thing as trying to be a good person or being nice to others or giving enough to charity to quiet the conscience or going on a short-term missions trip a couple of times? Every minute of today and tomorrow is given to you for the purpose of exalting Christ. You should plan to use them for their intended purpose. You should live on purpose, *this* purpose. Trying to be good to my fellow man is not the same as trying to help him as an expression of obedience to and love for Jesus. Going to a third-world country for a tough week of construction and VBS is not the same thing as seeking to take the gospel to the ends of the earth for the glory of Christ. It can be. But it can also be an exciting change of pace that makes us feel good about adding to our self-sacrifice quota. A Christian wants to be righteous because she loves Jesus, because he wants to please Jesus, because his or her only real goal in life is to honor Jesus.

Conclusion

When the world reaches its consummation, when our marriage to Christ is consummated, we will be pure, holy, sanctified, glorified, righteous, perfect, and a whole bunch of other sublime adjectives. We will be robed in virginal white. But we should start getting dressed now, in anticipation. We should ponder the coming of our Bridegroom-King and make ourselves as beautiful as possible for Him.

Part Two: Living Jesus First

8

Prayer

To this end also we pray for you always, that our God will count you worthy of your calling, and fulfill every desire for goodness and the work of faith with power, so that the name of our Lord Jesus will be glorified in you, and you in Him, according to the grace of our God and the Lord Jesus Christ. (2 Thessalonians 1:11–12)

Christians should pray for what Christ desires. We tend to pray for what we desire and for what we think others desire. We pray about finances, jobs, future spouses, safety, direction for making upcoming decisions, the details of planning events, and relief from pain and sickness. When praying for missionaries, we usually ask first for their security, provision, and health. In small groups and prayer meetings, we mention a potential relocation, a possible job transfer, trouble relating to a teenage daughter, struggle with the in-laws, or this new pain in the lower back area. These things matter to us.

Jesus didn't pray for such things, at least not in the prayers recorded for us in sacred Scripture. Consider the prayer of John 17. Jesus asked the Father to keep His disciples pure in the midst of a corrupt world. He asked that He sanctify them by His truthful word. He sought their unity among unbelievers so that the world would know that He had been sent by the Father. He asked that they would see His glory and be with Him forever. He prayed this way because His greatest concerns for them were Spiritual and eternal, not physical and temporal. Rarely can the same be said of His students two thousand years later.

The Lord's Prayer List

My high school football coach was known to invoke God's name now and then, but never in a, strictly speaking, religious sense. However, it always struck me that before and after every game he would lead the entire team in the Lord's Prayer. I remember having mixed feelings about it. On one hand, I knew that most of the guys saying the words did not know the God to whom they were speaking. On the other, it was moving to hear dozens of my teammates repeating those precious words in the context of a game. One thing that sticks in my mind to this day is that no one had to be taught the lines. They all knew the Lord's Prayer.

I'm sure you know it, too. But do you have a clear grasp of what our Lord taught the apostles to pray for? Temporal needs do show up in the request for daily bread. But it's not first. Or second. And percentage-wise, it's insignificant. The first request on Jesus' mind is that we regard our heavenly Father to be holy. Specifically, we are to pray that His name be holy to us. This is not the place to go into a full exposition about why that is important, but if you have never studied it, I urge you to do so. It's a wonderful and powerful endeavor.

I must ask, when was the last time you passionately petitioned the Lord to make His name holy in your life? How about in someone else's life? (Notice I'm not asking when you last said the words of the Lord's Prayer.) How often do you pray for this in comparison to health and other temporal needs? If it's first on Christ's list, don't you think it ought to find its way onto our list somewhere and with some sense of urgency?

The second request is that the kingdom of God come to the earth. Do you pray for that? Do you ask the Lord of heaven and earth to bring about widespread obedience across your neighborhood, community, nation, and world? Do you seek the One who can turn the hearts of kings to move them all to a willing obeisance to His glorious throne? We have already considered that all other kings are given their authority for the purpose of honoring the King of kings, and that none of the world's leaders are doing it. Jesus wants us to pray for them. Do we? The kinds of prayers I most often hear for national leaders are something like, "Lord, help our lawmakers and leaders to make decisions in accordance with your Word and will." I think what is usually meant is something like, "Keep them from legalizing abortion and homosexuality. Keep them from entering needless, unjust wars. And keep them from stealing our money through ungodly taxes." Now, don't get me wrong. Those are good things to seek. However, that is not the same thing as asking that the leaders make those decisions from a sincere desire to serve King Jesus. He did not teach us to pray for generally good morality in the land. He wants us to pray for their allegiance to Him.

After the daily bread comes the request for forgiveness. I would be willing to bet that most of us pray this one. But do we pray as our Lord instructed? He said, "Forgive us *as* we forgive others." It just got a lot harder. Do you pray for God to forgive you in precisely the same way in which you forgive those who have wronged you? Can you imagine how much less bitterness and conflict there would be in relationships if we all prayed this more often? Each time I ask this it causes me to do a quick inventory to determine whether I am holding a grudge against someone else. I desperately want God's forgiveness for all of my sins, so I need to make sure that I am extending that same amount of grace to others.

Then we are told to ask God either to keep us out of the evil one's path altogether or, if not, to deliver us from his schemes. The devil is out to destroy us or distract us individually, and to divide us corporately. He knows our weaknesses and greatest temptations, which he relentlessly seeks to exploit. As Jesus said to Peter, one-on-one with him we are no match whatsoever; he would sift us like wheat. And yet, how little time do we spend asking God to keep us from his enticing allurements? When did you last pray for a brother or sister to be protected from temptation? Which is more important in the long run, a mass on a friend's gall bladder or his marital loyalty in light of the attractive new assistant his boss just hired for him? There is no reason we cannot pray for both. But I fear that for most of us, the latter rarely gets asked at all.

Paul's Prayer List

Consider the content of Paul's prayers. In Ephesians chapters 1, 3, and 6, he sought the Father on behalf of his brothers and sisters for:

- The Spirit to grant them a greater knowledge of Christ
- An enlightened heart
- A deeper knowledge of the hope to which they had been called by God
- Their understanding of the riches of His glorious inheritance in the saints

- Their grasp of the immeasurable greatness of His power toward those who believe
- Them to be strengthened with power through His Spirit in the inner man
- That Christ would grow in their hearts through faith
- That they would know the love of Christ which surpasses knowledge
- That they would be filled up with the fullness of God

And he asked them to pray for him to be bold to proclaim the mystery of the gospel.

Do you pray like that? Again, how does your regular prayer list compare to this one?

We Pray For What Matters to Us

Since my first child was born, I have prayed for her to love Jesus and believe the gospel. But recently I realized that my prayers were more urgent whenever her life was in apparent danger; not prayers for her Spiritual health, mind you, but for her physical health. Now, as she drifts into her second decade of life and manifests daily the potential for just or unjust decision-making, I find a greater urgency welling inside to ask the Spirit of God to work in her heart for joyful, Christ-honoring love for Him above absolutely everything else. As the very real possibilities of Heaven or Hell, faith or unbelief, godliness or worldliness lay before her, my prayer concerns are vastly more focused and intense. Who cares if she lives on, only to perish when death finally wins? I must plead with the Mover of hearts to soften hers, or she dies eternally. Because I love her, I seek God for her ultimate good.

This exposes half of the reason we tend to pray for earthly things more than heavenly things: we don't love people like

Jesus loved them. We think that praying for a smooth flight is an expression of love. At one level it may be, but profound love seeks profound blessing. And there is no blessing comparable to a deep, passionate, consistent, faithful, accurate, strong, discerning, increasing knowledge and love of the Son of God.

Think of it this way: Jesus warned that if I love anything more than Him I am not worthy of Him, that not all who say "Lord, Lord" will enter the kingdom of heaven, that if I gain the world I lose Him. If you care about me, you will, above all, desire me to lose my life in order to save it. You, like Jesus, will say, "Who cares if Doug gains the world but forfeits his soul. I will pray for his soul." If you pray for my temporal happiness, prosperity, health, and the like, you may actually be praying for things that would tempt me to abandon Christ for earthly pleasure. Anyone who loves me will have the same urgency for my soul as I have for my children's.

The other half of the reason is that we don't love Jesus more than life. If Christ becomes our obsession, if His glory becomes our preoccupation, if His glory is our all in all, we will be obsessed with others becoming obsessed with Him. We will be preoccupied with others' preoccupation with Him. We will desire, more than anything else, that others glorify Him. Such a mindset would radically alter our prayer requests.

Praying and Persecution

I am comforted to find Paul asking for boldness. He often appears as Super Evangelist, brainier than an angry atheist, more logical than an educated Platonist, leaping goliath beatings in a single bound—the man of zeal. In reality, the regular anticipation of ending up in the hospital or prison of every town he enters would discourage even the bravest of hearts. No one dances into a room knowing he is about to receive thirty-nine lashes, at least not after the first lashing. Paul knew the temptation to soften the message in order to soften the blows. But his love for Jesus outweighed his love for himself. He asked the churches to pray for him to stand boldly in the face of intense persecution so that Christ would be exalted and the gospel proclaimed.

Other disciples shared this mindset. In Acts 4, when believers encountered the threat of punishment for their faith, they prayed not for relief but belief. They took the Scripture at its word. Psalm 2 had forewarned that the kings of the world would oppose Christ. Persecution was the expectation for all who desired to be faithful in this world of Christ-hating sinners. When it came, rather than release, they sought increased courage to fearlessly preach the gospel. More astounding still was the reaction of the apostles in the following chapter after being beaten to within an inch of their lives. Limping from the Sanhedrin's torture chamber, eyes and lips swollen, backs shredded, crusty with dirt and dried blood, there was no suggestion that God had failed to take care of them, no wondering about whether their friends had lifted them to His gracious throne. Rather, they rejoiced that God counted them worthy to suffer for the name of Jesus. They rejoiced in their suffering! We pray for its elimination. They loved the Lord and knew what the expansion of His kingdom required of them. We love ourselves and want the kingdom to grow with minimal pain or cost. Or perhaps though our rhetoric claims a devotion to His kingdom, our real devotion is to ours.

The worldview of the early disciples was not an enlightened, peaceful, philosophically justified society of progress, economic prosperity, technological advance, and medical miracles. They knew God was conquering the nations for His Son. They knew the nations would rage against His sovereignty. They knew that His servants were not above Him and therefore would suffer as He did. They knew the world would seek to attract their affections through the lusts of the eyes, the lusts of the flesh, and the boastful pride of life. They knew and believed. They considered the cost of discipleship and were willing to pay. They worked hard, not to avoid suffering and eliminate trials, but to love Christ through them. They prayed, not for ease, comfort, and sound bodies, but for endurance, patience, and sound minds no matter what God's providence brought to them. Our temptation is to escape pain and find pleasure. We are ever in the clear and present danger of becoming Christian hedonists (and not in the Piperisian sense).

Conclusion

Spurgeon attributed the success of his gospel preaching to the army of praying saints who sought the Spirit's transforming power during his services. Where are those praying saints today? Listen during this weekend's worship service to see which are the more prominent and frequent supplications at church—man's happiness or Christ's? Do pastors and worship leaders seek God for the things most important *to Him*? Is our greatest passion the exaltation and worship of the Lord Jesus Christ? Do we pray like it? When tragedy comes, do we forget that sometimes God causes blindness for the sole purpose of displaying His glory? Do catastrophes make us forget that the storms reveal the power of God, that only He can control them? Have disasters lost their ability to wake us from our spiritual slumbers? Are we deists at heart, no longer believing that this is our Father's world, and that the Father is first and foremost interested in His only-begotten Son? We are His only by adoption. The benefits of our adoption are vast and awe-inspiring, but we never outrank the Beloved. The universe exists for Him.

My kids pray for the things that matter to them, which usually includes food and fun. They ask for good times and good toys. I didn't teach them that, it came naturally. What comes *super*-naturally is the higher priority of the gospel and glory of Christ. Christians are to leave behind childishness and mature into full-grown sons and daughters of the living God. As we do, the content of our prayers will mature as well.

9

PREACHING

"For woe is me if I do not preach the gospel." (1 Corinthians 9:16)

The apostle Paul claimed to have only one sermon topic—Jesus and His cross. Most preachers today don't believe him. Either that or we find his diet insufficient and lacking flavor. Or maybe we fear that offering only Christ will lead to fewer mouths to feed because hearers tend to gravitate toward preachers who will tell them what they want to hear. Paul knew this, of course. He told his young protege Timothy to expect it. He warned that people would gather scratchers according to their itches.

Preach Christ or Nothing at All

Think of the various ways this can happen: A church loves doctrine. Red-blooded, masculine, hard-on-the-shins doctrine. Solid meat of the shoe-leather variety doctrine. No need to offer a sissy defense of free will there. They're men. Even the women. They take their Calvinism black and thick. What kind of pastor will they tolerate? A man who preaches the good news of the sovereignty and glory and power of almighty God. Any talk of grace, cross, or love must be carefully balanced with and subservient to the awesome ferocity of God's holy justice. They wouldn't want to leave any room for a wimpy, emotional, caring God. God cares for His majesty. And He is most pleased when His people spend the majority of their time analyzing and re-categorizing His glorious attributes. Doctrine is to be preached, debated, and defended. *That* is the mission of God's people.

I am being a bit facetious here, and I want to be careful. God is sovereign, glorious, powerful, almighty, and just. He is certainly not wimpy and must not be taken in a cavalier manner. No one knew this better than Paul. But he used the majesty of God's character not as an end in itself, but to exalt the wonder of His grace in saving sinners. He marveled that the ferociously righteous Judge of heaven and earth would show mercy to a blasphemer and persecutor of the Church, that He would give His own life to extend forgiveness to the chief of sinners, and that He would go so far as to call such a vile offender into ministry. Paul understood that the gospel was not an exposition of systematic theology, it was the message of grace and hope for wicked people. Paul preached Christ because Christ is all.

Another church loves doing good, especially to the community around them. Their passions include providing food for the hungry, building homes for the homeless, sending clean water to poverty- and disease-stricken lands. They love to find creative ways to make others feel important and accepted. They are convinced that nobody wants to hear a story about Jesus unless they first see the story of His love lived out by His people. So, this church will seek a preacher who calls them to a relentless pursuit of sacrificial giving, and who leads by example. They want to know how to be better neighbors, better co-workers, and better friends. They want their teacher to teach them and show them.

Jesus did teach that the world would be able to identify His disciples by witnessing their acts of kindness . . . *to one another.* How easily we forget that it's our selfless devotion to the family of God that will impact unbelievers more than our devotion to them. More to the point, however, we must remember that the gospel is about sin and our desperate need for forgiveness.

Who cares if we help a family avoid foreclosure so they can all go to Hell in a nice house? You may say that the family would care, at least in the immediate future. True enough. But what about the long-term? Do we care about that? To what degree? Moreover, there is nothing uniquely Christian or Christ-exalting or gospel-minded about helping the poor. A card-carrying atheist can do that. More moreover, Jesus did not come to eradicate trouble in this life but to deliver us from the eternal death we deserve in the next. We eviscerate the work of Christ by making it mostly about the temporal needs of vile, rebellious, God-haters. When Jesus cried out, "It is finished!" He wasn't talking about food stamps.

Preach the Gospel at All Times . . . With Words!

Please don't hear what I'm not saying. I'm not suggesting that believers should be unconcerned with trying to make the world a better place. I'm only asserting that our highest and most articulate concern must be Christ. The old adage, "Preach the gospel at all times and when necessary use words," is nonsense. The gospel cannot be preached without words because it is a story, a report, a message. It's not a lifestyle. Paul commanded Timothy to "preach the word," not "fix the bicycle."

A faithful preacher will proclaim Christ to his audience relentlessly, incessantly, and unapologetically. If nobody wants to hear that message, so be it. There is no other.

I want to reiterate that the word to be preached is the gospel of Jesus Christ. Some might be lulled into thinking it's Grudem's *Systematic Theology* or Warren's *Purpose-Driven Life* or Piper's *Desiring God*. As good and helpful as some of these may be, the Christian preacher preaches *Christ*. On the Lord's Day, we proclaim the Lord. When we utter, we make utterances about the wonders of God's glory as revealed in and through Jesus Christ. We proclaim *Him*!

Having only one sermon does not require us to say the same thing every time we speak. Our task is to preach the gospel accurately and effectively, and it's not very effective to leave one's audience bored stiff. Exalting Christ is never a dull enterprise. We shouldn't express it as such.

Effective preaching requires creativity, fresh insights and approaches, helpful illustration and application. We must preach with passion, as those who have been impassioned. We must be Christ-obsessed ourselves if we are going to stimulate others to be. We must know our audience and excite in them a thirst for the pure milk of the word of the cross. None of this is merely rote or routine, lifeless or limp, drab or dull. What could be more inspiring and invigorating than discovering new ways to call God's people to praise the glory of His magnificent grace? Our message is always the same—Christ and Him crucified. If that's insufficient or uninteresting to you, you have no business preaching.

Temptations for preachers are multifaceted and strong. We are easily attracted by our pet doctrines. They become our hobbies, our free-time reading and pondering. At first, they are scattered here and there in our sermons, but over time they become more prominent, dominant even. We also like to know that our preaching is making a difference in people's lives. We feel the strong pull to make people feel good, useful, and encouraged, so we strive to make our sermons beneficial. Or maybe we want to make profound theological statements, spurring God's people to reflect on the deeper, more mature things of God. Or maybe we so passionately desire holiness for our people that we give them a steady diet of rules and standards, making sure that they grasp just how far off the mark they still are. And then there's the ever-present lure of application. We must figure out how to create that epiphanic, life-changing, *aha!* moment that will give our people a new way to look at things.

But our preaching exists for the same purpose as everything else—to exalt Christ. These other things must be secondary to and directly derivative of our presentation of His glory.

We preach that which interests us or that which we find in the text. Christ must be what interests us and what we find in the Bible. Anything else is distracting. If the gospel is not our greatest hobby, we shouldn't be preaching. If we can't figure out how to make the gospel relevant to people's lives, we shouldn't be preaching. If we don't find the gospel to be the most profound theological concept in Scripture, we shouldn't be preaching. If we don't find the gospel to be enough motivation for righteous living, we shouldn't be preaching. If the mercies of the gospel leave us the same two days in a row, we shouldn't be preaching. If we get bored by, unimpressed with, or tired of the gospel, we shouldn't be preaching. Preach Christ or don't preach at all.

Preaching the Christian View of Same-Sex Sin

Does this mean there's no place for preaching on practical issues, theological issues, cultural/societal/political issues, moral issues, etc.? Of course not. But all of these must be postured according to how they relate to exalting Christ.

Take the same-sex marriage issue, for example. There are two ways to oppose it: We can sound the alarm about the coming doom to civilization and culture as we know it. We can decry the breakdown of the family. We can pull out the statistical data showing the negative impact on children when both genders are not present in the home. Or, we can argue like Christians, declaring that marriage is intended by God to be a picture of Christ and the Church, a picture which cannot be pictured without a man and a woman.

Let me explain further. "Same-sex marriage" is a meaningless concept. It's like two people holding only gloves and saying they're playing a game of catch, or putting two nuts on a piece of metal and claiming to have bolted it down, or holding two halves of a bun and calling it a hamburger. Same-sex marriage is like that. Without both genders, something essential is missing. I'm not talking about reproductive organs (though that is certainly true), I'm talking about the essence of what makes marriage marriage. Although people of like gender are clearly capable of having orgasmic experiences and committed affection with each other, what they cannot have is marriage because its purpose requires more than sex and vows. Ultimately, it's not a civil union or a state issue. It's a Christ issue. God established it at the beginning of human existence not merely to lay the foundation for the family and society, but, far more importantly, to foreshadow the marriage between the Son of God and His Wife (Eph. 5:31-32). This is why there will be no marriage in the next age. The shadow will give way to the substance. Marriage will serve its intended purpose and then pass away. Therefore, the rationale for defining marriage as a relationship between a man and a woman is only secondarily about preserving civilization or the family. The *primary* reason is because marriage pictures Christ and His bride, the Church. The husband is to stand as the Christ-representative exercising headship, authority, cherishing, nourishing, and sacrificial love, thereby mirroring Christ's responsibility; the wife is to represent the Church exercising submission, respect, admiration, honor, and devoted love, thereby mirroring the Church's role. You cannot have this picture with two men or two women.

When preachers speak against it, we tend to fight more as human beings or American citizens or natural philosophers than as Christians. We argue that with same-sex marriage the family is at stake, or that a well-ordered society requires both parents in the home, and so on. But there is nothing uniquely Christian in those conclusions. A well-educated atheist might make the same claims. The *Christian* opposition employs an argument that unbelievers must deny because the true significance of marriage is something they must deny.

Like everything else, marriage was created for Christ, and we must debate as Christians rather than as Americans, conservatives, or philosophers. Otherwise, we fail our King, and we help unbelievers in their efforts to steal it away from Him.

Practical Christian Preaching

The same is true when it comes to sermons defending or denying eternal security, admonishing employees not to waste their employer's time, describing whether wives may work outside the home, instructing believers on how to think about taxation, or explaining whether Christians may rightfully serve in the military. All of these things matter because they relate to Christ, His glory, His inheritance, and His people. When the New Testament speaks to them, it's always in the context of the supremacy of Jesus Christ. Regardless of the subject, a sermon which fails to preach Christ fails to be a Christian sermon.

Some will probably object to this by suggesting that a Christian politician, for example, cannot simply rise on the Senate floor and reject a marriage bill on the grounds that it distorts the image of Christ and the Church. He would first be laughed at, then castigated for uniting church and state. He must be content to take incremental steps and to debate from the common ground we have with unbelievers. I appreciate the intent behind such thinking. But, in the final analysis, he would be merely speaking as an American politician who also happens to hold Christian values. If a person fails to claim Christ as the rationale for marriage, he is not positing a Christian argument. He may be arguing as a republican, a philosopher, a historian, or as a founding fathers advocate, but not as a Christian. As an American citizen, I am all for prohibiting homosexual marriage by any rationale, but the only thing that authoritatively rules it out is its relation to High King Jesus.

I recognize that according to its title, this chapter is supposed to be about preachers, not politicians. But there is overlap. Any congressman who claims to be a Christian will belong to a church and place himself or herself under elder authority. Preachers need to instruct them on how to live for Christ on Capitol Hill. The government has been telling us that we are (mostly) free to teach what we want in the privacy of our church buildings, but when we leave the parking lot we must leave our religion behind. We are free from religion in

America. King Jesus didn't vote for that. He claims the American king as His subordinate, and He's asked us to reveal that to him. Who is in a better position than the Senator himself? And who will tell the Senator? The preacher.

Conclusion

The apostle Paul suffered every kind of oppression, affliction, and rejection because of his unwavering commitment to preaching the gospel. It cost him everything, humanly speaking. It gained him everything, heavenly speaking. After fighting the good fight of the gospel, he received his wreath from Jesus Himself. But before his Day of reward, he urged Timothy to fight the same fight for the gospel, to be ready in season and out of season, when the ground is soft and when it is hard, when people love to hear it and when they hate it. At all times and in all places, this one sermon is to be the all-consuming passion of the preacher. There will always be the temptation to be accepted, to be found clever and funny, to get a reaction from the hearers, to appear prepared and competent, to gain a following, and a million other things. Preachers must resist them all. The call is to proclaim Christ and to motivate others to love and live for Him.

A Final Note to All of Us as Hearers

What kind of preaching attracts us? What do we gravitate toward or push against? What kind of diet do we crave? By what standard do we critique preachers? If Christ's glory and gospel are not the center of our attention and desire, we must re-align. Just as preachers should have only one sermon, so also hearers should seek only one sermon. Idolatry is never very far away from any one of us.

10

FAMILY

"Let your fountain be blessed, and rejoice in the wife of your youth." (Proverbs 5:18)

Marriage

Labor of Love?

As Larry and Lisa approached the midway point of their first decade as Mr. and Mrs., they each began to realize some things about their relationship. It wasn't what they thought it would be. It wasn't what they hoped it would be. It wasn't what it started out to be. It mostly wasn't.

Larry was disappointed by Lisa's disinterest in him. She rarely asked sincere questions about his job. She rarely smiled at him. Rarer still was her interest in using the bed for anything other than sleep. She complained more and more all the time. She kept herself very busy. And maybe the most painful of all was her constant belittling, carping, and nagging. She wasn't a happy woman.

Lisa was lonely. She felt neglected. She felt like Larry's roommate, his maid, sometimes even his prostitute. He could get very excited about his work, his team, and his golf, but his wife bored him. She noticed how he would talk for hours with his friends, but transformed into the world's greatest one-line-manufacturer when intercoursing with her. Oh, and, intercourse with her couldn't have been further from his mind if he lived on Pluto.

Then someone recommended a couple of books, and they began to realize that their expectations were way out of biblical whack. Marriage is not about happiness, it's about holiness, they learned. They had been looking for love in all the wrong places. Silly them, they were searching the *love & intimacy* sections when they should have been looking under *character development*. Suddenly it all made sense. They had a renewed vision for their marriage. They had new ambitions. They had hope.

Larry began to pray earnestly to lose his desire for her partnership in life. He didn't want to be selfish that way. He sought to bless her and be kind to her with no thought of what she was or wasn't doing in return. He prayed for contentment. He prayed for patience with her complaining and nagging. He prayed for the gift of encouragement so he could help her in all the activities *she* was pursuing. And he prayed for a radical reduction in his sexual yearnings. No longer pursuing happiness, he now only wanted to be sanctified by their marriage.

Lisa's seeking was similar. She sought comfort in her solace, constantly reminding herself that Jesus was her all-sufficient companion. She prayed for joy in serving her neglectful husband. She retrained her thinking to find pleasure in offering her body to him, even if he didn't show any interest in taking it.

She encouraged him to spend more time with his friends, more time at work, and more time watching ESPN. She, too, wanted only to be sanctified by their marriage.

Larry and Lisa had finally found the secret of a godly marriage: *lower expectations.* They would no longer expect any happiness except the happiness that comes from disappointment. They would no longer expect any pleasure except the pleasure that comes from sacrificing. They would no longer expect any companionship except the companionship that comes from solitude.

Mere Marriage?

If that's the secret to marriage, then somebody should tell all of the spouses-to-be. Quick! Tell the future wives to set aside their dreams of a close friend, a romantic lover, and a lifelong cherisher. Tell the future husbands to set aside their pursuit of a willing helpmate, an encouraging admirer, and a passionate pleasure-partner. Marriage is about sticking it out. It's about self-denial. It's about endurance. It's about long-suffering. It's about the painful process of becoming more righteous and selfless. Doesn't that sound great? No wonder people are getting married all the time. Who wouldn't long for that kind of relationship?

I'm being a little facetious. But only a little. Such a view of marriage simply doesn't do justice to the biblical portrait. Is there no sweetness in the Savior? Is there no delight in the Deliverer? Is there no happiness in the Holy One? Of course there is. He is our abundant life. He prepares a banquet in our honor. In His right hand are pleasures forevermore. He sees us, knows us, fills us, rejoices over us, and delights in us. Union with Christ is surely more than happiness, but it is not less. And it is *that* union which human marriage represents.

We must remember that just like everything else, marriage was created for Christ. And just like everything else, it exists for His supremacy. But a dichotomy which pits holiness against happiness is unnecessary and can lead toward a "grin and bear it" attitude as if we should simply resign ourselves to the fact that it's for our good (kind of like going to the dentist).

As a picture of Christ's love for His people, marriage is certainly a sanctifying tool. But it was not intended to be drudgery. It was designed to be more than merely tolerated and survived.

God's Design for Marriage

Here's the point: If you are married, your relationship exists to exalt Christ. Yes, you do that by pursuing holiness. But that is not unique to marriage. What is unique to marriage is the husband's responsibility to show his wife how wonderful Christ is, how lavish His grace, kindness, generosity, gifts, romance, pleasure, strength, security, and blessing are. This, of course, requires him to become increasingly holy and selfless, but not merely for his own sanctification. He must seek *her* good, *her* joy, *her* delight. He is to show her Christ's love.

Larry must not remain content with mediocrity. He must give Christ first place in his marriage by being Christ to his wife. He must love, cherish, nourish, provide for, protect, and sanctify her. That's his role and calling as a husband. Lisa must also put Christ first in their marriage by representing the Bride of Christ. She must respect, honor, and admire Larry. She must seek to help and encourage him. She must pursue relational and sexual intimacy, seeking to know and to be known. She must join him in showing one another the glory of the grace of Jesus. There is no mere resignation in that kind of ambition.

They will both be grinning alright, but not as a result of merely bearing with one another.

We know this instinctively. It's not simply cultural inculcation or tradition that form the great wonder and anticipation two people experience on the day of their wedding. Brides and grooms dream big. They imagine glorious days ahead in which they can finally be together in wedded bliss. Even in a fallen world, our matrimonial imaginations run wild.

Why? Because if there is any situation in which a person ought to enjoy the benefits of Jesus Christ, it's in the very relationship given to exemplify His gracious love. Consider that the Spirit of God inspired an entire book on the topic of marital pleasure. To be sure, the *Song of Songs* sings of that which is holy, righteous, and good. But it's also that which is intensely pleasurable, alluring, and desirable.

When marriage fails to deliver, it's because one or both of the partners have failed to be intentional in exalting Christ. A browbeating, inattentive, abdicating husband does not exalt Christ. Nor does a rebellious, loose-lipped, withholding wife. Nor do two people limping along, trying to get by and avoid divorce or adultery. Marriage was created to glorify and honor Jesus Christ. Every couple should strive for nothing less than that.

Christ Can Make Your Marriage More Christ-Like

I will readily admit that marriage provides regular opportunities to become more holy and more selfless (all the more so for my beloved wife). And I understand that God's will for our lives is our sanctification. But in marriage, one of the most significant elements of our holiness should be our anticipation of eternity with Christ, our everlasting blessedness.

A Christian marriage shows itself as set apart from worldly marriages when it mirrors this blessedness. Consider a man who shows great self-restraint at the constant verbal bludgeoning he receives from his wife. He doesn't slap her in response, and he genuinely wants to love her in spite of her sin. Does that reflect Christlikeness? Of course. But he should do that with *every* woman. She is not every woman, she is his wife. His desire should be for them both to enjoy an earthly foretaste of heavenly bliss. Currently, their marriage tastes bitter. He should be praying for the Spirit of God to show him how to be Christ to her, whether that requires him to rebuke her (always messy and never fun), teach her (always involving hard work), romance her (always difficult when dealing with a bludgeoner), or go to pastoral counseling with her (always hard on the ego). Certainly, he should pray for holiness, self-control, self-denial, and so on. But his primary concern should not be self. He didn't marry her so that he would become holy. He married her because he loved her, and the most loving thing he can do for her is to help them have a marriage worthy of Christ. *He* is what marriage is all about.

If your response to this is, "Yeah, that sounds good, but you don't know my spouse," or "It's too late for us, we're too far down the river," or "Our marriage could never be that wonderful," or "I'm broken, damaged goods, there's no hope for me," let me remind you who Jesus is. He's the one who spoke the universe into existence. He's the one who tells the oceans to go this far but no farther. He's the one who tells every lightning bolt where it should go. He's the one who made a worshipper out of Abraham, a leader out of Moses, a psalmist out of David, an apostle out of Saul. He is in the business of changing hearts, attitudes, ambitions, thoughts, and passions. If His Spirit can make you love Him, He can make you and your spouse love each other. Why would He not want to do that in your marriage? Is yours the one exception, the one relationship about which He doesn't care whether it accurately reflects His love for the Church? Seek Him, ask Him, plead with Him, work with Him, love Him, and believe Him. He loves marriage, even yours.

Parenting

In the Fear and Admonition "of the Lord"

Our goals as Christian parents must be more about Christ's aims than society's. If our kids make it to their mid-20s or so having avoided major embarrassment and jail time, we feel pretty good about ourselves. If they have a decent job and an above-average spouse, we feel very good. Such ambitions may be admirable by cultural standards, but they are paltry for believers in the Lord Jesus. Remember, our children were created for Him. They exist to glorify Him. They were entrusted to parents to teach and show them how.

Raising children in the fear and admonition of the Lord involves more than simply telling them to shun evil and do good. We fail if our sights are set any lower than the crown on Christ's head. For example, lying is not to be avoided because it can get a fellow in trouble or because one falsehood leads to another and another until it's one big mess. Lying is unworthy of a person who lives to serve the Truth. A person who wants to exalt Christ will speak words that edify and encourage, things lies don't do. Likewise, pre-marital sex is a distortion of Christ's committed love for His people. And stealing is unbecoming to those who know the One who gave His life for their salvation. And he who loves Jesus will seek to be controlled by His Spirit rather than drugs and alcohol. And laziness prevents the proper devotion the King deserves from His subjects. And...see the point? Christ's supremacy is our goal, not nice boys and girls who stay out of trouble.

This is not to say that college, jobs, and marriages are unimportant. But they must be seen and encouraged from the vantage point of what gives Jesus first place. A man does not have to be a preacher nor a woman a missionary to exalt Him. But their paths of life should be chosen according to those trajectories which point most clearly to His throne. If a boy shows giftedness in business, his parents should teach him to use his resources and entrepreneurial genius purposefully for Christ's glory. A young woman should be encouraged in her desires for marriage, but not simply so she can settle down, live a good life, have a nice home, and enjoy the American dream. She should seek a man who wants to partner with her in praising Jesus explicitly in all that they do.

Christian character should take priority over skill development (without neglecting the latter). Teaching a child to express love, show grace, serve others, refrain from grudges and revenge, speak truth, remain loyal, and other virtues should be at the top of our lists as parents. Instruction in how to study God's Word, how to participate in corporate worship, and how to pray should predominate. And none of these should be presented with a "check-box" motivation. They aren't to be done because they're the "right things to do." They should be expressions of allegiance and worship to the Lord Jesus. They are ways to demonstrate an obsession for Christ like a hug demonstrates an affection for a sister.

I haven't said anything unknown or revolutionary here. Yet, my observation of parents reveals that very few are willing to exert the necessary and painstaking effort required to raise kids who are devoted to exalting Christ. It's much easier to train in life skills and acceptable behavior. We are noticeably proud of the athletic or intellectual accomplishments of our kids, while leaving the hard work of Christian education to pastors, or teachers, or chance.

Why Parents Should Discipline Their Children

When your child acts selfish, does it shock you? When he disobeys (again!), are you surprised? Do you set aside your belief in the sinfulness of all mankind when the "all" includes your kid? We should be surprised when the little reprobates *do* obey. But more to the point, how do you react when a child breaks *your* rules? Does it provoke anger? irritability? impatience? Are you frustrated that she would dare contradict *your* authority?

If so, you are not thinking Christianly. The only reason a father has authority over his son is because God has given it to him. And there is a specific outcome expected from that authority. Children are to be taught how to please Christ. So, the real tragedy of a rebellious daughter is that she is turning against her Lord, not her mother. The task of the mother is to turn her back. The fact that disobedience is disruptive to mother's plans is irrelevant. Ultimately, mom is just a servant, too. Her appropriate service is to help her child learn to see Christ's worthiness of love and worship.

Singleness

"Being single..." for some it means freedom and fun. For others it means loneliness and longing. For both, it should mean greater opportunity to serve Christ. Marriage and family are wonderful gifts, but they also demand our time and attention in huge amounts. A person without these demands is free to apply more energy to ministry, edification, and so on. Her longing should be to serve Christ more fervently and extensively.

Single men and women who use their "extra" time to hone their rock climbing skills should go back and read 1 Corinthians 7 again. The Bible's perspective is apparent. They have more time to seek out ways of honoring Christ. Their ambitions should be directed toward giving Him first place. They have extra time to serve in formal church ministry, more time to enjoy true fellowship with other believers, more time to study and teach, more time to meet with a discouraged brother and point him to hope in Christ, more time to spend proclaiming the gospel to unbelievers, more time to use their gifts for the benefit of Christ's people. All other pursuits must be secondary and squeezed in through the cracks of purposeful, Christ-exalting efforts.

Conclusion

Much more could be said about marriage, parenting, and singleness, but I hope this is enough to get you to think about how to be intentionally Christ-obsessed in each of them.

11

Mission

"Then He opened their minds to understand the Scriptures, and He said to them, 'Thus it is written, that the Christ would suffer and rise again from the dead the third day, and that repentance for forgiveness of sins would be proclaimed in His name to all the nations, beginning from Jerusalem.'" (Luke 24:45–47)

As I write this, the term *missional* is all the rage in many Christian circles. For all the rhetoric, I'm not entirely sure what is meant by it. Some use it in non-threatening ways. Others have basically replaced the gospel with it, not only in terminology, but also in content by making the Christian's benefit to his local community the highest priority.

Whatever else may be said about it, the *biblical* priority is clear. And any person, movement, or organization that does not set proclaiming the gospel and exalting Christ as the highest priority is off mission. Community service, helping the unfortunate, disaster relief, acts of mercy and compassion, etc., are all good, but they are not the specific and unique call of the Church. Unbelievers can do them. The government can even do them (although with more expense and less effect). What only Christians can do is preach Christ. That is our mission.

Evangelism

Do you know what the gospel is? Could you take someone to a passage in the Bible which clearly and succinctly explains it? Hopefully, your mind has gone to 1 Corinthians 15 where the apostle lays it out simply and concisely. Let's take a stroll down this lovely path stopping to look at a few of the salient features.

> Now I make known to you, brethren, the gospel which I preached to you, which also you received, in which also you stand, by which also you are saved, if you hold fast the word which I preached to you, unless you believed in vain.
>
> For I delivered to you as of first importance what I also received, that Christ died for our sins according to the Scriptures, and that He was buried, and that He was raised on the third day according to the Scriptures, and that He appeared to Cephas, then to the twelve. After that He appeared to more than five hundred brethren at one time, most of whom remain until now, but some have fallen asleep; then He appeared to James, then to all the apostles; and last of all, as to one untimely born, He appeared to me also. (1 Corinthians 15:1–8)

First, notice that the gospel was *preached*. It was not demonstrated through acts of kindness, nor shared like a virus. It was spoken, compellingly so.

Second, salvation requires the believer to *hold* to the gospel, to *stand* in it. This is no quick, emotional prayer. This is devotion and persistence. Conversion is an enduring change. To abandon the gospel is to abandon salvation.

Third, Paul considered the gospel to be the highest priority. It was *of first importance*. It was his preeminent concern for the church at Corinth. No cause or pursuit held a higher place in his mind, and he wanted all Christians to have the same perspective.

Fourth, the gospel is about Christ dying for our sins. If the Church loses the significance of sin and Christ's atoning death, it loses the gospel. The good news is only good in contrast to the bad news. The bad news is that we have rebelled against God thereby incurring His just punishment. Your friends, neighbors, coworkers, and relatives may need a lot of things, but what they need above all is for their disobedience against God to be forgiven. That's what the gospel message is about.

Fifth, the gospel includes both the death and the resurrection of Jesus. As Paul goes on to teach in this chapter, if Jesus is still dead, we have no hope. There is no good news without a living Christ. I got into a small debate with a seminary mate of mine one time about whether it would destroy Christianity if the body of Jesus was found. My argument went something like this, "If, hypothetically, we discovered the remains of a human being and could somehow prove infallibly that it was Jesus of Nazareth, I would cease being a Christian immediately because without an empty tomb we have an empty faith." He countered with something about how the triune nature of the Godhead demanded the incarnation and resurrection, and therefore, it couldn't be Jesus' body. I said, "But hypothetically, for the sake of the argument, let's say we did find His body. Would you still believe in Him?" He said he would. I think that is nonsense. The resurrection is part and parcel of the gospel, and without it we have nothing. Without it, Jesus was a fraud.

Finally, we shouldn't miss that twice Paul uses the phrase, "According to the Scriptures," once in reference to His death and once in reference to His resurrection. Why, in such a terse summary, does he say it twice? Because believers need to understand that the death and resurrection were God's plan all along. He had predicted it throughout the Old Testament, and now the mystery was revealed. It was not a new plan or a change in plans or a Plan B. Jesus was the lamb slain before the foundation of the world. Rather than be surprised or disturbed by His death and resurrection, we should see it as the fitting and expected climax to God's purposes throughout history.

Is this the gospel you believe? Is it what you proclaim to unbelievers?

Let me ask another question. If an unbeliever wanted to know what law he had disobeyed that rendered him guilty before God, how would you respond? There probably isn't one uniform answer. Some would jump immediately to the Ten Commandments and charge him with violating several of them. If you knew him well, there might be plenty of evidence readily available such as lust, bitterness, gossip, or greed. But I suggest that there is an even better approach. Why not go straight to the biggest offense—his failure to believe the gospel and love Christ. He may be able to weasel around the others, claiming that he doesn't lust while looking at pornography, or he has forgiven his brother, or he is just concerned about others, or he's saving up to help the poor. But his loyalty to Jesus will either be clear and avowed or not. He will either confess Jesus as Lord or he won't. If he does, but his life says otherwise, it is easy enough to remind him that Jesus said: "If you love me, you will keep My commandments." Since exalting Christ is his created purpose in life, call him to repentance starting there.

Paul's gospel preaching in Acts 17 is a great example for us. When he began evangelizing the pagans in Athens, he went straight for the death and resurrection. He didn't build relationships or try to be a good witness and hope someone would notice. He didn't put on his fish t-shirt with a well-crafted summary of a Bible verse. He proclaimed Christ. When he had the attention of some, he explained that he knew the one God they didn't know, and that this God, maker and ruler over heaven and earth, would judge everyone by the Man, Jesus Christ whom He raised from the dead. In essence, he was preaching that one day they would all bow to Jesus and confess Him to be Lord. Better to do it now while there is hope of forgiveness.

We don't like to talk about sin, our own or anyone else's. We've been told for so long that to charge others with sin is arrogant and judgmental that we are starting to believe it. But there is a difference between preaching Hell and hellish preaching. To confront a person with his or her failure to honor Christ is the single most loving thing we can do for them, if we do it as one fellow sinner to another. It only becomes arrogant when we condemn with a condemning attitude. The gospel is about sin, and we will never help someone find their only hope of salvation if we don't talk about it.

Missions

Recently, a young man came to me with a great ambition to promote missions in our church. He had several ideas about how to stir interest in missions, raise funds for missions, solicit prayer for missions, and recruit people to go on missions trips. I appreciated his zeal. However, I told him that if we were to proceed with some or all of his plan, the rhetoric would have to change. *Missions* would not be the focus, Christ would.

John Piper articulated it exceptionally well when he said that missions exists because worship doesn't. Calling humanity to worship Christ is our "job."

Christ gave the original job description, and we would do well not to improve upon it. He commanded the Church to make disciples in every nation (Matt. 28:18-20). That's the mission before us, should we choose to accept it.

Missionaries must be about the business of making followers of Christ or they fail to be *Christian* missionaries. It seems silly to even have to make this point. Yet, there are myriads of temptations which can keep a missionary off mission. Strategic relationships being initiated or planning meetings being held or coffee shops being built can all generate great excitement and appear like missions work. But if they don't transfer to actual proclamations of the gospel, they fall short. Don't get me wrong, I understand and appreciate the need for planning, relationship building, and so on. I'm not suggesting that missionaries should always just ride into town and hop on their soapbox. But it does concern me when missions reports are full of all sorts of testimonies except the gospel being preached or when prayer for missions is mostly about logistics.

Conclusion

Our primary motivation for taking the gospel to the world should be obedience to our Lord's command and a desire to see all nations obey Him, not the lostness of man. In other words, missions is primarily Christ-centered, not man-centered. But notice that I said *primarily*. We should care about fellow human beings who are currently on the path of destruction. Love demands it. And love for Christ demands it. Still, Jesus is the reason for everything, including the salvation of sinners.

12

LOVE

"If anyone does not love the Lord, he is to be accursed. Maranatha." (1 Corinthians 16:22)

We judge a man not by what he believes or hopes, but by what he loves. That was Augustine's astute observation long ago. It's an easy statement with hard impact.

Words, as they say, are cheap. A man may claim incomparable wealth without actually having a dime to his name. A kid may tell his friends all about his awesome vacation to Disney World, even if it never actually happened. A would-be messiah may say that your sins are forgiven without actually having the authority to grant it. The proof of the pudding, as they also say, is in the eating.

This is precisely what James was getting at in his faith and works discussion. Anyone can *say* he believes the gospel, even a well-trained parrot. The proof comes as the professed faith works out. If it's genuine, it will show itself. Real faith is not hidden under a basket, it's a city on a hill which cannot be missed. The kind of faith wrought by the Spirit of God produces a living, active love for the Son of God. Faith that has no life is, well, dead. Dead faith doesn't save anybody.

Neither is hope a good indicator of a man. Any man can hope. We can be utterly convinced in our minds of just about anything. I mentioned earlier the false prediction of Christ's return. Camping's was just one of many such failures. Yet that didn't prevent some people from quitting their jobs and heading to the mountaintops for a bird's eye view of Jesus as He came riding the waves of the sky. They did this *in hope*. They were wrong. Their hope had no substance, no foundation, no reality. While their heads were in the clouds, their feet had no ground beneath them. We can't test a man's commitment to Christ by whether or not he hopes to have eternal life. There will be many on that day to whom the Lord will say, "I never knew you." Their hope was hopeless.

But love is different. Love reveals what is real in a man.

We Love Ourselves

When the serpent came to Eve, he didn't appear one day and say, "It's either me or God. You will serve one of us, which will it be? You must choose." If that were his approach, he would have made a more majestic display, dressing as a lion or a dragon or something provoking more fear and awe than a snake. But he knew better. Given the choice between serving him or God, the woman would have picked God no matter how impressive his own show might have been. But if the choice was between serving God or serving *herself*, his chances of success where greatly improved: "*Your* eyes will be opened, Eve. *You* will be like God. *You* will know good and evil..." and now the woman begins worshipping her true love. "Hey, that fruit could be good food for me. That fruit looks good to me. That fruit can make me wise. *Bon appétite!*"

Our greatest natural love is for ourself. Does a husband neglect his wife out of love for *her*? Does a mother speak critically to her daughter out of love for *her*? Does a boy disobey his father because he loves *him*? Does a couple break fellowship with its church family and seek to undermine its integrity in the community due to their love for *the church*? Does a man lash out in anger toward his boss out of love for *him*? Does a person harbor bitterness against another because of love for *them*? No. All of these and many, many more arise out of a love for self. We get hurt because we are concerned with ourselves. (There's a reason it's called *self*-pity.) We commit adultery because we love ourselves. We criticize, demean, and cutdown others because we love ourselves. We betray a friend because we love ourselves. We grow impatient, annoyed, and bothered because we love ourselves. We refuse to do the hard things of life because we love ourselves. We become lazy, cynical, and introverted because we love ourselves. We fail to love others because we love ourselves.

You might say that we come by this honestly because the world constantly commands us to be true to ourselves, take care of number one, do what makes us happy, and make our own way. Don't be naive. It's not an American invention. It's not a product of the 60's. It's not new. It goes all the way back to the Garden of Eden. And it has always been successful because my primary concern is me, yours is you, and Eve's was Eve.

Satan really only employs one strategy. He has only one. He exploits our love for self. Take that away, and he is powerless. Peter loved himself enough to deny the Messiah. Judas, enough to kill Him. But consider the Messiah Himself. The devil searched and searched for the selfish crack in Jesus' armor, but there was none to be found. He offered food after 40 days of starvation. He offered extensive power. He offered validation and certainty about God's love for Him. But Jesus loved God and man more than Himself, even to the point of death on the cross. Satan's head was crushed. The snake was defanged, its venom neutralized. It was finished.

Do you see why the two greatest commandments involve love? Do you see why all other commandments hang on these two? What sin would you ever commit if you loved God with all your heart, soul, strength, and mind? In what way would you offend your brother, sister, husband, wife, son, daughter, mother, father, friend, neighbor, coworker, fellow church member, or sales clerk at Walmart if you loved them?

But how will you ever love God or your neighbor if your greatest love is yourself?

Another Kind of Love

I said our greatest *natural* love is for ourself. There is a super-natural love, a love created by the Spirit of the God who is Himself love. When the Spirit gives new life to a human being, He produces love for God and others. He changes the object of our affections and desires. He leads us to love someone other than ourself.

The Greatest of These Is Love

What is love? Do you know? It's not a feeling, though it involves our emotions. It's not a tradition, though it forms habits. It's not a language, though it must be expressed. Love is sacrificing what is yours for the good of another. It's denying your own interests so that others will be satisfied. It's dying so that others may live. It's His will, not yours, be done.

Love remains patient when its own wishes are not met by others. It acts kindly toward others, treating them as a brother or sister in all circumstances. It does not become jealous of others, but rejoices in their blessings. It does not boast in its own accomplishments. It does not seek attention for itself. It doesn't do things that are inappropriate. It seeks the pleasure and fulfillment of others, not its own. It doesn't become upset or hurt by others. It forgives all of the sins against it. It is not aroused by wickedness. It dances when truth is believed. It endures all trials, believes through all circumstances, hopes in all that God has promised, and remains steadfast to the end. Faith may be lied about, hope may be misdirected, but love never fails. It is real. It lasts. It is greater than all. A man will be judged by what he loves.

Love Tells the Truth About Your Faith

Jesus said that if you love Him you will keep His commandments (John 14:15). Notice He didn't say that if you love Him, you *should* keep His commandments. He didn't leave room for a person to convince himself that he loves Jesus while failing to obey Him. This is a cause and effect relationship. The one who loves Jesus *will* obey Him; the one who doesn't obey Him doesn't love Him.

A few verses later, He said that the person who keeps His commandments is the one who loves Him, and that whoever loves Him will be loved by His Father (John 14:21). We see again that God is preoccupied with people loving and obeying Christ. That's why they exist. Do you want God to love you? Do you want fellowship with God? Do you want to live in the presence of God? Love His Son, the Lord Jesus Christ. There is no other way. To reject Jesus is to reject God. Love Jesus with all your heart, soul, strength, and mind. He is your Lord.

So, our love for Jesus is demonstrated by our obedience to His commands. What does He command? He commands us to love one another. And here we are brought to the heart of new covenant ethics—our love for others, especially believers, proves or disproves our love for Jesus. It's all over the New Testament, but most saliently in John's writings. If you don't love your fellow Christian, then you don't love Christ. It's that simple. If you are not patient, kind, and forbearing with other believers, you don't love Jesus. If you are jealous of them, inappropriate around them, upset by them, and bitterly begrudging toward them, you don't love Jesus. If you seek what's best for you and work for your own pleasure rather than that of your brothers and sisters in Christ, you don't love Jesus no matter what you say you believe about the gospel, and no matter what hope floats in your dreams. You will be judged by what you love because what you love says everything that needs to be said about what you really believe.

How Love Grows

Take care not to be drawn down by the innate gravitational pull toward works-centered obedience. Its weight is intense. The goal is not good works, it's love. We must focus on loving Jesus, and strive for a greater fervor and passion for His glory, rather than create a list of do's and don'ts. Only increased love will lead to increased obedience. It's the circumcised heart, not the circumcised foreskin, that serves God faithfully.

How do we increase our love for Jesus? There are two ways:

First, we seek the power of God's Spirit. Love is His fruit. We have already discussed it: He can change our hearts. He can move what moves us. He can increase our desire to please Christ. He can give us the zeal of John the Baptist to want more of Jesus and less of ourselves. He was sent to glorify Christ. He will do it through you. You should ask Him to, in faith without doubting, in hope and great expectation, incessantly and desperately. He will do it. He promised.

Second, we magnify our sin and His forgiveness to their accurate proportions. Earlier in the book, I mentioned Jesus' statement that he who is forgiven much loves much. So, if you want to love Jesus more, be forgiven more. That's not an encouragement to go do a bunch of heinous things so that His grace may abound. God forbid! You've already done enough heinous things. But for most of us, by the time we are finished minimizing the true wickedness of our thoughts, words, and deeds, a high-powered magnifying glass is required to see it.

People put certain sins in the category of *wicked* wickedness (unless, of course, *we* have committed them, in which case they get put in the other one). Such malevolent monstrosities are: murder, rape, incest, child-molesting, adultery, and similar abominations. Others we place in the category of *not ideal, but nobody's perfect* wickedness (what Jerry Bridges effectively calls "respectable sins"). These include: critical, harsh, biting sarcasm; refusal to accept encouragement and kindness from others; abdication of love and discipline in parenting; a wife's refusal to submit to her husband; a man's failure to cherish his wife; parents who have routines but no relationship with their children; withdrawing from fellowship because one feels left out or unwanted or taken for granted or hurt; a teenage boy's devotion to video games; a teenage girl's devotion to teenage boys; lack of commitment to a church body; interpreting situations according to our feelings rather than according to truth; and a host of others.

But is it really a *small* thing for a husband to pursue his work, hobbies, and buddies to the neglect of his wife? Is it "not that big a deal" for a wife to withhold herself emotionally and physically because she doesn't feel appreciated or understood?

Is it "probably wrong, but what are you going to do?" when a father demonstrates rigidity and justice without grace, or neglect and cowardice without responsibility? Is it understandable that a pastor would be more concerned about getting caught watching porn than being incompetent with the Word of God?

And then there are the sins we “deal with” all the time such as giving social networking priority over Bible study, failing to truly pray, offering complaint rather than gratitude, speaking words that tear down rather than build up, and coming to worship while longing for football or a nap. These we don’t see as significant. We’re just "tired," "unaware," "struggling," "having a hard time right now," "afraid," and "too busy." We justify our sin with extraordinary skill.

In order to grow in our love for Christ, we must be honest about the depth of our depravity *and* the extent to which we love ourselves more than we love others.

But magnifying our sins to their accurate size will only produce pain, despair, and anger if we do not also magnify the grace of our Savior to its accurate size. We must believe the gospel. We must accept our full acceptance in the Beloved. We must immerse ourselves in the incomprehensible love of Jesus.

Too often, people will wallow in their own wickedness, refusing to believe the gospel for themselves. They feel too sinful or too inconsistent or too late for Christ to truly forgive them. They choose to let their own interpretation and evaluation overrule His. Again, it's the *self* who rules, and it's nothing less than unbelief and lovelessness toward Christ. It's saying to Him that His sacrifice was not enough, that the cross was insufficient: “It may be good enough for others, but I'm too ruined. It'll take more to redeem me. I'm a special case. ”

Excuses, justifications, self-condemnations, and escapism dominate as such a person lives in unbelief and self-exaltation.

Genuine, saving faith admits the truth of sin *and* forgiveness. It sees the magnitude of Christ's love and condescension in taking human flesh in order to serve vile rebels. It revels in the One who traded glory for Hell so that we could trade Hell for glory. It believes in the cross. It believes in complete forgiveness. It believes in grace greater than all my sin. It believes.

Then it loves.

13

Why Did I Write This Book?

Because I Needed to Read It

I heard or read an author (I think it was Douglas Wilson) explain that he wrote books because *he* needed to read them. That is certainly the case here. I needed to think "on paper" about how Christ is the center of and motive behind everything that God is doing in the universe. I must be taught again and again that the Bible is the story of Jesus and no one else. The words, "Jesus is Lord," flow easily from my lips, but to wrap my mind around the enormity of that statement, and to set my heart beating for its appropriate end, required a fresh and careful meditation. I know the Bible is about Jesus, but to keep knowing it I must learn it over and over. That's why I wrote this book.

Because I Couldn't Keep It In

You know that sensation when something strikes you as particularly funny and you can't stop thinking about it? And you can't stop laughing about it? And you can't stop your mind from gravitating to it? And the next several hours or so are marked by sudden outbursts of chuckling and giggling? You try to repress it. You try to put your mind somewhere else. You try to get on with your life, but for the rest of the day you are controlled by the cackle. That's sort of what has happened to me. Only it's no laughing matter, nor has it waned after a few hours.

Since discovering *and understanding* that all things were created for Jesus, it just comes out of me, in casual conversation, in counseling meetings, and certainly in preaching. I am constantly thinking about how this points to Christ, or how that calls for allegiance to Christ, or how this would change if our objective was the glory of Christ. And then, with spontaneous and irresistible force, I find myself speaking of Christ. I see Him everywhere in the Bible. I see "made for Jesus Christ" stamped on the clouds, the mountains, and the squirrel in my backyard. I hear Him as the lyric of the world's song, and I must sing.

And I must write.

Because Christ Is Life (Colossians 3:4)

Jesus isn't a helpful add-on to life. He isn't simply our comfort and hope. He is life itself. Eternal life is knowing Him (John 17:3). Without Jesus, you have no existence and no meaning. With Jesus, you have these abundantly and endlessly.

Many years ago, Thomas Brooks wrote, "He enjoys nothing, who lacks communion with God; he lacks nothing, who enjoys communion with God; therefore above all gettings, get communion with Christ, and above all keepings, keep communion with Christ." We cannot truly delight in anything if we are far from the Savior. On the other hand, when our fellowship with Christ is sweet, everything else tastes sugary as well.

I have written hoping to help you find that incomparable savor of living for the Savior.

Because You and I Must Exalt Jesus as King

I have used the phrase *intentionally Christ-obsessed in all things* repeatedly throughout this book. It's the phrase I hope will accurately characterize my life. I say "hope" because I have not yet been able to achieve it with any permanence. But I will keep trying, for He is worthy.

Each word is carefully chosen. I want to be taken, preoccupied, and entirely consumed with Jesus Christ. I want this obsession to extend to every aspect of my life, big or small. And I want my zeal for Christ to come deliberately, with premeditation and forethought. Pleasing Christ is not something one stumbles upon or does accidentally. It is to be the highest, most constant pursuit of any person's life.

The reason I want to be obsessed with Christ is simple, it's because God is obsessed with Christ. He made the universe so that His Son Jesus would be exalted to its throne. I have written in the hope that you will join me, as I join King David, in proclaiming to Christ:

> "Yours, O LORD, is the greatness and the power and the glory and the victory and the majesty, indeed everything that is in the heavens and the earth; Yours is the dominion, O LORD, and You exalt Yourself as head over all." (1 Chronicles 29:11)

Amen!

Douglas Goodin is the senior pastor of Front Range Alliance Church (www.frontrangealliance.org) in Colorado Springs, CO. He is also the founder and president of *Cross to Crown Ministries* and the *New Covenant School of Theology*. Doug, his wife Krista, and their three children are blessed to live with a clear view of the majestic Pikes Peak from their kitchen window.

Cross to Crown Ministries exists to motivate Christians to be intentionally Christ-obsessed in all things. Our motivation statement reads, "Numerous causes compete for the allegiance of Christians. Some are good things, others border on idolatry. The Scripture, however, declares that Christ is to have first place in all things (Col. 1:18). Therefore, we work to encourage believers toward purposeful living with explicit devotion to Jesus Christ in every facet of life (whether Bible study, teaching, marriage, parenting, worship, working, playing, learning, retirement planning, or anything else we do)." We produce written, audio, and video resources to this end.

We also train pastors, elders, leaders, and intentional Christians at the *New Covenant School of Theology*.

Information is available at: www.crosstocrownministries.org.

Made in the USA
Charleston, SC
05 March 2012